PRINCIPLES
OF PRESBYTERIAN POLITY

PRINCIPLES OF PRESBYTERIAN POLITY

CARLOS E. WILTON

Geneva Press
Louisville, Kentucky

© 2016 Carlos E. Wilton

First edition
Published by Geneva Press
Louisville, Kentucky

16 17 18 19 20 21 22 23 24 25—10 9 8 7 6 5 4 3 2 1

Book design by Sharon Adams
Cover design by Allison Taylor

Library of Congress Cataloging-in-Publication Data

Wilton, Carlos, 1956-
  Principles of Presbyterian polity / Carlos E. Wilton.
    pages cm
  Includes bibliographical references and index.
  ISBN 978-0-664-50345-1 (alk. paper)
  1. Presbyterian Church (U.S.A.). Book of order. 2. Presbyterian Church (U.S.A.)--
Government. 3. Presbyterian Church--Government. I. Title.
  BX8969.6.P743W55 2016
  262'.05137--dc23
                                                            2015031514

♾ The paper used in this publication meets the minimum requirements of the American National Standard for Information Sciences—Permanence of Paper for Printed Library Materials, ANSI Z39.48-1992.

For Claire

CONTENTS

Part 2: Principles   27

FOREWORD

The *Book of Order* states that "[t]he Church is the body of Christ. Christ gives to the Church all the gifts necessary to be his body. The church strives to demonstrate these gifts in its life as a community in the world" (F-1.0301).

The key concepts are gifts to be the church and the demonstration of the gifts as a community. The *Book of Order* is how the Presbyterian Church (U.S.A.) has organized itself to demonstrate its gifts as a community. It is just a book with words. But those words shape us and push us until, as the proverbial teacher says, we have lived up to our potential.

After an effort of almost ten years the Presbyterian Church (U.S.A.) approved a revised Form of Government in 2011. This revision was the result of thousands of conversations, historical and social research, and brave vision casting. The vision was to have a Form of Government (FoG) that allows for the multiple contexts of congregations and presbyteries: contexts as varied as the Presbyterians-packed Pennsylvania and the sparsely populated Wyoming, contexts as varied as New York City and Salina, Kansas. Very different contexts exist in a presbytery with 35,000 members and a presbytery with 3,500 members. The former Form of Government created a structure that required uniformity. As the country and the church changed, that uniformity did not serve the mission of the church.

A multiyear committee project led by the late former moderator Cynthia Bolbach brought forth a revision that met this challenge. It separated the foundational material of what we are as Presbyterians from the governance material. There is now a Foundations of Polity section in the constitution. This section spells out a clear articulation of who we are as Reformed people and how we are shaped as a church. It combines historical material with ecclesiastical prose.

One of the most noted differences in the revised Form of Government is that it starts with the mission of the congregation. In G-1.01 it states in part: "The triune God gives to the congregation all the gifts of the gospel necessary to be the Church. The congregation is the basic form of the church, but it is not of itself a sufficient form of the church." These two sentences both spell out the need for a contextual witness where each congregation lives out its mission to its community. A congregation with many gifts to meet the many needs of its community. But it also says that we are a larger church who shares gifts and strengths among its congregations. What is the impact of what seem contradictory statements? The impact is that we are church together. The gospel may be shared to twenty in worship or to two thousand. A congregation may have a once-a-week food pantry or a community nutrition program. It is all a common and yet unique effort. These efforts become sufficient to the mission of Christ's church because we share the gifts of Christ together.

The revision of the Form of Government in 2011 leads the church into a new century with a vision of the whole and the particulars, in that we keep our Reformed mindfulness to equip individuals to be thinkers and doers of mission and honor the collective wisdom of councils. It is the Reformed way.

Gradye Parsons
Stated Clerk of the General Assembly
of the Presbyterian Church (U.S.A.)

ACKNOWLEDGMENTS

I am grateful to the Rev. Fred Anderson, my first seminary field education supervisor, who led me through my first study of the *Book of Order*; to the Rev. Richard Armstrong, who taught me polity in seminary; to the Rev. William Chapman, whose writings and example have led me to understand the *Book of Order* in light of the Historic Principles and who provided helpful comments on an early draft; to David Maxwell, editor at Westminster John Knox Press, for his valuable counsel; to my polity students at New Brunswick and Princeton Theological Seminaries, who provided practical suggestions after using the manuscript in class; to colleagues from the Presbytery of Monmouth and the people of the Point Pleasant Presbyterian Church, who graciously allowed me time to finish the project; and most of all to my wife, the Rev. Claire Pula, for her love and support through it all.

INTRODUCTION

A Matter of Principle

It was past 10:00 p.m., and still the fierce discussion around the session table dragged on. Irene's fellow ruling elders had been at it for nearly an hour, and she was despairing that agreement would ever emerge.

Two factions were on a collision course: those who were backing a capital campaign to renovate the sanctuary and those who were not. One group, eager to create an open chancel appropriate to the church's growing informal worship service, favored the campaign. The other side, deeply attached not only to traditional worship but also to the beloved space where so many family members had been baptized, married, and commended to life eternal, thought it a bad idea.

Irene had friends on both sides. She knew how dug-in each faction was, how reluctant they were to concede even an inch of ground. In their own way, each side believed the future of their congregation hung on this decision.

In her distress—without even waiting for Harry, her pastor and session moderator, to recognize her—Irene blurted out: "Can't we all just get along?"

There was a moment of stunned silence. Then Frank, the author of the renovation proposal, sneered: "You can't be serious: *that* old line?"

Victoria, Frank's staunchest opponent, surprisingly agreed: "The time for getting along has passed. One side's got to win this thing, once and for all!"

Irene retreated into silence. She felt sorry she had even opened her mouth.

But then Pastor Harry spoke up. "Irene's got a point. Although she may not realize it, she's echoing one of the deepest principles on which our Presbyterian government is based. Let me read you a few lines from the *Book of Order*: "We also believe that there are truth and forms with respect to which men of good characters and principles may differ. And in all these we think it the duty both of private Christians and societies to exercise mutual forbearance toward each other" (*Book of Order*, F3.0105).

"Those lines were written," Harry continued, "not long after the Revolutionary War. Only men exercised church leadership back then. Those men-only days are thankfully long behind us, but the church has kept that historic language just as it was written. That's because the principle of mutual forbearance—the art of deeply listening to one another in times of disagreement, and finding ways to get along—is so central to who we are as Christians. This is what the *Book of Order* calls a preliminary principle: one of the things we Presbyterians say we believe, on which all other rules are based."

The pastor's words changed the tenor of the debate. Both sides still argued their strong views, but they took Harry's reminder to heart. The session now realized that, as a council of Christ's church, their meeting had to proceed differently than that of the local town council or neighborhood association. One opinion would prevail in the end. There was only one sanctuary, after all, and either it would be renovated or it would not. Yet the session members now realized they could make that decision in a way that honored the deeply held convictions of all parties.

It had become, for them, a matter of principle.

To the Reader

You may be a newly elected ruling elder in the Presbyterian Church (U.S.A.). You may be an experienced ruling elder, following a presbytery-required course of study before being commissioned to particular service as a supply preacher. You may be a seminarian preparing for ordination as a teaching elder. You may be a ruling elder recently elected by your session as a commissioner to presbytery or a teaching or ruling elder elected by your presbytery as a commissioner to synod or General Assembly. Or you may be an experienced ruling or teaching elder seeking to brush up on your polity knowledge. If you fit any of these categories—or if you are simply curious to know more about how decisions are made in the Presbyterian tradition—this book is for you.

All readers should note that, as of the time of this writing, the General Assembly is about to consider a proposal for a new Directory for Worship that would entirely replace the present one, thereby rendering this book's Directory for Worship paragraph citations (those beginning with the letter "W") obsolete. Should that proposal be approved by the General Assembly and a majority of the presbyteries, the new numbering system would take effect in June 2018.

Why a Book of Order?

A Manual for Mission. Most people, opening the *Book of Order* for the first time, feel a little intimidated. With its unfamiliar terms and oddly numbered paragraphs, the book resembles a law book. "That's not what I signed up for!" may be the initial response.

At the heart of the Presbyterian faith is a Lord of love, not laws. The carpenter of Nazareth calls disciples to fish for people, not to follow procedures. The first inclination may be to dismiss church governance—this thing Presbyterians call "polity"—as a necessary evil at best and a "dismal science" at worst.

That would be a huge mistake. The *Book of Order*—the product of the collective wisdom of generations of church leaders—has been written not to impede Christian mission, but to advance it. Properly used, the *Book of Order* is a manual for Christian mission. Paul's letters reveal how very common it is for a Christian community struggling to discern God's will to become mired in conflict. We all know that, when Christians fight with one another, Christ's mission is the loser.

The first chapter of the *Book of Order* affirms that "Christ alone rules, calls, teaches, and uses the Church as he wills" (F-1.0202). Yet who speaks for Christ? There's the rub. Without ordered decision-making processes that broadly spread the work of discernment among church leaders, the loudest, most narcissistic voices will likely prevail, to the detriment of the gospel.

Reformation Roots. Among other things, the Protestant Reformation was a rebellion against centralized, monarchical authority in the church. Searching the Scriptures and the writings of ancient theologians, John Calvin—the Reformation's brightest intellectual light—discerned an older tradition of governance. This tradition was built on the decisions of councils: assemblies of elected church leaders. It was Calvin's deep conviction that communities are better equipped than individuals to discern the leading of the Holy Spirit.

As Calvin's Presbyterianism made its way to the New World—an arduous ocean voyage away from the established national churches of Europe—his theological heirs came to realize they needed new ways of being the church. They reinvented Presbyterian government for the New-World context.

In the absence of princes powerful enough to impose church government from above, they rebuilt their quintessentially American church order from below. Their innovation was in tune with the needs of Colonial America: Presbyterian governance would help inspire the uprising that became the American Revolution. Some described the Revolution, on the floor of Parliament, as "that Presbyterian rebellion."

First Principles. The first principles of this American adaptation of Presbyterianism are displayed in the Foundations section of the *Book of Order*, specifically the third chapter (F-3.01). Two important chapters precede this one: a chapter grounding the mission of the church in the authority of Jesus Christ, its head (F-1.0), and a chapter relating church government to the first volume of the *Constitution*, the *Book of Confessions* (F-2.0).

Having grounded its authority in Christ and the Confessions, the *Book of Order* goes on to present two sets of foundational principles: the 1788 Historic Principles of Church Order (F-3.01) and the 1797 Principles of Presbyterian Government (F-3.02). These two lists are different from one another in purpose. The first is more theological in nature, the second more practical.

Note the difference in the names of the two lists. The first has to do with order; the second, with government. The first addresses the *why* of church order; the second, the *how*. Order is a divine gift. Government is a human construction. Order is the manner of life God intends for humanity. Government is humanity's practical method of carrying out that mandate.

The Principles of Presbyterian Government (F-3.02), although modeled on the eighteenth-century original, were extensively rewritten as part of the revision process that led to the present Form of Government.

As an analogy, consider the world of music. On the one hand, there is music theory, the study of first principles such as pitch, rhythm, and harmony; these principles are organized (in the Western musical tradition) according to the eight primary notes of the scale and are measured by conventional time signatures. On the other hand, there is musical practice, which involves arranging the fundamental musical elements into a pleasing composition. Few composers achieve greatness without first grounding their creative vision in solid theory.

In the life of the church, proceeding directly to the *how*—while giving the *why* a mere wink and a nod—is a sure route to stifling legalism. That is why this study of the *Book of Order* takes its form from principles rather than practice, order rather than government.

There are two ways to learn Presbyterian polity. The first is through rote memorization. The second is a more inductive method, by which students first master the general principles in the Foundations section of the *Book of Order*, then track those principles as they are replicated in the chapters that follow. This book follows the second method.

Those with the patience to attend to "first things first" will find in these pages an enduring but adaptable model, centuries old, of how the Presbyterian expression of the body of Christ orders its mission and ministry.

Tracing the Hidden Structure. The *Book of Order* is a lean, elegant, and highly logical document. With the Historic Principles of Church Order (F-3.01), the Principles of Presbyterian Government (F-3.02), and the other foundational documents as the starting-point, subsequent chapters build upon those that precede them.

This is analogous to the way reinforced-concrete buildings are designed.

Such buildings are constructed of concrete blocks laid one atop another, row upon row. The new structure rises predictably, its architectural footprint replicated in the stories above.

Concrete blocks are solid, with open spaces at their inner core. As masons stack the blocks, they line up the hollow, inner spaces to form a series of silos. Then they drop long, iron bars, known as rebar, through the empty columns. Finally, they fill the remaining space with poured concrete. The result is a strong and durable structure, able to resist not only the downward tug of gravity but also the side-to-side pull of other physical forces.

Theological themes rise through the *Book of Order*'s structure like rebar rods, lending stability to the higher levels. Students who comprehend the basic theological footprint are often able to predict what the later chapters will say, even before they consult them.

It is especially important to be aware of this orderly, sequential structure in this era of hypertext documents. As electronic versions of the *Book of Order* increase in popularity, more users are accessing its material using electronic search technology or by clicking on hypertext links in other documents. This is like entering a building through the upper-story windows rather than through the ground-floor entrance lobby. While swift and convenient, this approach sometimes causes readers to miss the big picture.

Presbyterian Polity DNA. The concrete-block analogy has its limitations because the Bible portrays the church not as a static structure but as a living organism, the body of Christ. A biological analogy may serve us better.

One of the greatest advances in the history of biological science occurred in 2003, when a team of researchers published an essentially complete sequencing of the human genome. The Human Genome Project, a fifteen-year joint effort of the United States Department of Energy and the National Institutes of Health, gathered the findings of a multitude of scientists from around the world into a complex map of the forty-six chromosomes of the human body and its more than 20,000 genes. This biological map is guiding the work of countless medical researchers.

The organizational structure of the Presbyterian portion of the Christ's body is likewise built around a genome of sorts. Like the double-helix chromosome of human DNA, it is comprised of two intertwined and complementary patterns: the Historic Principles of Church Order and the Principles of Presbyterian Government. Learn those principles, and the practice follows naturally.

A Fresh Approach

In writing this book, I am deeply indebted to a fellow student of polity and a mentor of mine, William E. Chapman, who was my predecessor in teaching Presbyterian polity courses at New Brunswick and Princeton

Theological Seminaries. His book *History and Theology in the* Book of Order: *Blood on Every Page* (Witherspoon Press, 1999) has guided earlier generations of polity students in understanding the Form of Government in a similar systematic fashion.

Following the major revision to the Form of Government in 2011, a revised guidebook is needed. More is required than simply updating specific citations that have changed. The present Form of Government, leaner and more flexible in its specific applications, differs in so many ways from its predecessor that it calls for a fresh approach.

In part 1, we will set the *Book of Order* in the context of other sources of authority in the church and will go on to highlight some of the ways the *Book of Order's* language and organization set it apart from other books. After those preliminaries, we will move on, in the second and third chapters of part 1, to examine the first two chapters of the Foundations section, which acknowledge Christ, Scripture, and the Confessions, in that order, as higher sources of authority in the church. We will round out part 1 by setting the Historic Principles in their historical context.

In part 2, we will consider each of the Historic Principles of Church Order in turn, making connections between them and specific practices—primarily from the Form of Government and the Rules of Discipline. In the final chapter of part 2, we will briefly examine the Principles of Presbyterian Government.

PART I
Preliminaries

Chapter 1

BECOMING FAMILIAR
WITH THE BOOK

In order to become familiar with the *Book of Order*, it helps to understand the nature of its authority in the church and also to pick up some basic navigation tips and terminology. It is also useful to know what major changes came along in 2011 with the adoption of the present Form of Government.

You Can Tell This Book by Its Cover

The first thing to notice, upon picking up the *Book of Order*, is the cover. Along with the title there is a subtitle: The *Constitution of the Presbyterian Church (U.S.A.), Part II.* Part I is an entirely separate volume, the *Book of Confessions.*

How are the two volumes related to each other? Section F-2.02 aligns the Scriptures, the Confessions, and the *Book of Order* in order of priority: "These confessional statements are subordinate standards in the church, subject to the authority of Jesus Christ, the Word of God, as the Scriptures bear witness to him."

No sentence in the *Book of Order* is more important than this one. It displays a clear hierarchy of authority. First, there is Jesus Christ the cornerstone, the living head of the church. Second comes the most foundational of the church's documents, the Scriptures—"Where that Word is read and proclaimed, Jesus Christ the Living Word is present by the inward witness of the Holy Spirit" (W-2.2001). Third comes Part I of the *Constitution,* the *Book of Confessions*—a digest of the theology expressed in the Scriptures as interpreted in the Reformed tradition. Finally, there is Part II of the *Constitution,* the *Book of Order,* which specifically applies Scripture and Confessions to guide the life of the church.

The *Book of Order*'s cover also displays a range of two years, reflecting the General Assembly's biennial meeting schedule. New editions of the book are

It is worth noting that the *Constitution*'s prominent mention of Jesus Christ as the living head of the church discourages any excessively literalist interpretation of the Scriptures. Literalist interpretations, while paying lip service to the lordship of Christ, tend in practice to lift the authority of the written Word of God over that of Christ the living Word.

3

necessary because each General Assembly recommends to the presbyteries that the *Book of Order* be amended in a variety of ways. Once those amendments have been ratified by a majority of the presbyteries, they are included in the next edition of the book, marked in boldface type. A new edition is prepared as soon as a majority of the presbyteries have spoken on all the amendments recommended by the previous Assembly.

Naming and Numbering

Opening the book's cover and moving on to its Preface, we discover a brief description of the contents of Part I and Part II of the *Constitution*. The Preface lists each of the confessions included in the *Book of Confessions* and then explains that the *Book of Order* is divided into four sections:

- Foundations of Presbyterian Polity (F)
- Form of Government (G)
- Directory for Worship (W)
- Rules of Discipline (D)

The letters F, G, W, and D are prefixes that precede each numbered paragraph of the *Book of Order*. Readers who come upon a citation from the book can instantly find the section from which it comes.

The *Book of Order* contains page numbers for convenience, but serious students of polity consider the page numbers to be a secondary feature. The paragraph numbers are of greater importance, because they do not generally change as the book is amended. Also, the historic rulings of permanent judicial commissions gathered in the *Annotated Book of Order* specifically cite paragraph numbers.

The *Annotated Book of Order*, available from the Office of the General Assembly in both print and electronic versions, provides the full text of the book, interspersed with citations referring to judicial rulings and actions of the General Assembly.

On occasion, an amendment may remove an entire paragraph. In such a case, the other paragraphs are not renumbered. Typically, the old number is retained with no text beside it, other than a historical notation that begins: "[This section was stricken by . . .]." This is necessary because older citations in judicial decisions may direct readers to a paragraph that is no longer part of the book.

A final caution: paragraph numbers utilize decimal points after each principal section number, with further numbers added off to the right, as needed. Unlike decimalized numbers in mathematics, zeroes have value in this system. Thus, 1.0 precedes 1.9, but 1.10 follows 1.9 (in mathematics, the sequence world be 1.0, 1.10, 1.9).

Precision in Language

Next comes a brief glossary of commonly used words. Wherever these words appear within the book, they have a legally precise meaning. Readers are well advised to become thoroughly familiar with the specific definitions attached to each of these words, because they are applied consistently throughout the book:

- "Shall" and "is to be/are to be" signify practice that is mandated.
- "Should" signifies practice that is strongly recommended.
- "Is appropriate" signifies practice that is commended as suitable.
- "May" signifies practice that is permissible but not required.
- "Advisory handbook" signifies a handbook produced by agencies of the General Assembly to guide synods and presbyteries in procedures related to the oversight of ministry. Such handbooks suggest procedures that are commended but not required.

In particular, it is important to fully internalize the difference in meaning between the frequently occurring words "shall" and "should" or "may." The difference here is between mandatory and optional. The bottom line is this: "shall" allows absolutely no wiggle room, while either "should" or "may" opens a loophole that allows situational discretion.

Important Changes in Terminology

Next comes a list of outmoded terms that no longer appear in the *Book of Order*, along with their replacements that appeared for the first time in the 2011–2013 edition. In 2011, a completely new, simplified Form of Government replaced the former edition, which had grown in size and complexity over the years as the result of numerous amendments. With that new edition:

- "Minister" or "minister of the Word and Sacrament" became "teaching elder."
- "Elder" became "ruling elder."
- "Governing body" became "council."
- "Commissioned lay pastor" became "ruling elder commissioned to pastoral service."
- "Office" or "ordained office" became "ordered ministry."
- "Officer/s" became "[person/those in] ordered ministry."

An explanation of the reason behind these changes is in order, since some of the older terms continue in everyday use among those reared on earlier editions of the *Book of Order.*

Two Types of Elders

The 2011 Form of Government's most far-reaching terminological change was its substitution of "teaching elder" for "minister of the Word and Sacrament," and its corresponding substitution of "ruling elder" for "elder."

Throughout the history of the three principal antecedent denominations of the Presbyterian Church (U.S.A.)—the Presbyterian Church in the U.S.A., the Presbyterian Church in the U.S., and the United Presbyterian Church of North America—there have been two different systems of nomenclature for presbyters. Prior to the 1983 reunion, the elder/minister pairing was stronger in churches whose heritage lay with the former northern denomination, the United Presbyterian Church in the U.S.A. The teaching elder/ruling elder variation was favored in many churches of the former southern denomination, the Presbyterian Church (U.S.).

The title of "deacon"—an order of ministry that is optional, according to G-1.0201—continues to be used without controversy, although in some parts of the former Presbyterian Church in the U.S., the word was historically used for those overseeing the congregation's financial affairs, rather than those exercising caring ministries of "compassion, witness and service" (G-2.0201). Both understandings of the distinctive diaconal functions grow out of Acts 6:1–7, in which seven men are set aside to "wait on tables" of the widows and orphans being fed by the church. The Greek original of that phrase can therefore be understood to refer to either face-to-face compassionate service or the management of the common purse that makes such service possible.

There are advantages and disadvantages to each. The "minister of the Word and Sacrament" title more accurately describes the tasks most commonly performed by those serving as pastors of congregations. Moreover, it reflects the two Reformed "marks" or "notes" of the church identified by Calvin: proclamation of the Word and celebration of the sacraments. The word "minister" is also the standard in most other churches of the Reformed tradition, including the Church of Scotland, and is more intelligible to ecumenical partners outside the Reformed tradition.

The disadvantage of the elder/minister pairing is that it can make the church more vulnerable to clericalism. Such language may lead some to give ministers of the Word and Sacrament priority in church governance, since both Calvinist marks of the church are included in their position's title.

The chief advantage of the ruling elder/teaching elder formula is that it gives clear expression to an important principle of Presbyterian polity: the parity of the two orders of ministry that share governance responsibilities. According to this principle, church councils above the level of the session are composed of equal numbers of both.

Another advantage of the ruling elder/teaching elder pairing is that, by removing the word "minister" from any single order, it encourages its application to all three orders on an equal basis. This gives voice to the under-standing that servant ministry (*diakonia*, in the Greek) is the motivating spirit behind all forms of Christian ministry.

John Knox added a third mark of the church, the administration of ecclesiastical discipline, although this mark—being associated with councils rather than individuals—is not exclusively associated with the pastoral order of ministry. The teaching elder/ruling elder variant began not with Knox, but with the Scottish Reformation's second-generation systematizer of Presbyterian governance, Andrew Melville. It never caught on in Scotland but achieved some popularity on this side of the Atlantic.

The chief disadvantage of the ruling elder/teaching elder pairing is that it does not accurately describe the multitude of tasks performed by teaching elders. It raises one function—teaching—above all others. This is especially problematic with respect to the celebration of the sacraments. As Reformed liturgical theologians are energetically raising the profile of the Lord's Supper by encouraging more frequent celebration, the change to "teaching elder" may appear to signal a step backward.

Significantly, "teaching elder" does not reflect the trend of many decades of broadening the functioning of individuals ordained to that order of ministry. A century ago, nearly everyone ordained to this function served as the sole pastor of a local congregation, preaching frequently. In larger congregations today, there are associate pastors who seldom preach or teach. Presbytery rolls also include a multitude of specialized ministers (chaplains, counselors, administrators, and the like) for whom teaching is not central to their day-to-day functioning.

As far as the order of ruling elder is concerned, the adjective "ruling" is one that requires continual explanation and interpretation, in contrast to the plain sense of the term (see F-3.0202). Most casual observers today understand "ruling" to refer to either monarchical domination or a formal legal opinion issued by a judge. Each of these suggests an individual style of governance that does not reflect the collegial Presbyterian decision-making tradition.

Finally, it can be questioned whether the move to the ruling elder/teaching elder terminology elevates governance to exaggerated importance, with respect to who Presbyterians are as a denomination. No other Christian denomination names its ordained leaders according to their role in church governance. Eastern Orthodox, Roman Catholic, and Episcopal priests bear a title (priest) that points to what they do at the altar, interceding between the worshiping congregation and God. Lutheran, Methodist, and Baptist pastors bear a title (pastor) that points to their role in shepherding God's people. Congregationalists and others from the Reformed tradition retain the title of minister, elevating to prominence the servant-of-the-Word spirituality to which their leaders aspire.

For those who prefer an alternative to the ruling elder/teaching elder language, the Form of Government does retain the title of "minister of the Word and Sacrament" as a secondary option (G-2.0501). Outside the setting of parliamentary meetings, a great many Presbyterians continue to use the more universally recognizable titles of "minister" and "elder."

The Coming of Councils

Another linguistic development in the present Form of Government is that "governing bodies" have become "councils." This particular generic category—comprising all the various levels of governance—has proven chameleon-like over the years. Originally, Presbyterians spoke of "courts" of the church (giving particular emphasis to their role in adjudicating disciplinary cases). As disciplinary cases both decreased in number and came to be handled by commissions—rather than by councils meeting as committees of the whole—that term morphed into "judicatories." In the Form of Government crafted after the 1983 reunion, "judicatories" became "governing bodies."

The present term of choice, "councils," is a term with a rich pedigree. It reaches back to the early centuries of the church, when ecumenical councils such as those meeting at Nicaea and Constantinople rendered far-reaching decisions. In more recent times, the First and Second Vatican Councils played a similar role within the Roman Catholic tradition.

Although this change sent the committees once called "councils" scurrying to find a new name for themselves, this term succeeds in grounding Presbyterian practices of communal governance in a larger ecumenical tradition.

Ordered Ministry

The final significant change in language is from "office" or "ordained office" to "ordered ministry." The term "office" as applied to Reformed ministry has long been problematic, because the word carries connotations of individual decision-making authority. This official conception of ordination attains its most distinctive form in certain Roman Catholic and high-church Anglican circles that understand the essence of ordination as conferring an "indelible mark" on the recipient. The indelible mark persists for life, unless ordained status is removed by a specific disciplinary procedure colloquially known as defrocking. In that way, ordination is analogous to baptism, which Christians of all traditions see as conferring an indelible spiritual mark.

It has never been entirely accurate to speak of Presbyterian ordained offices. Reformed theology of ordination is a functional understanding, not an official one. The church ordains men and women to service because there are tasks to be done, and these are best fulfilled by someone set apart by the laying on of hands, with prayer. The laying on of hands grounds the ordination in ancient practice but must never be seen as instrumentally transferring a special ordination charism.

The indelible-mark theology of ordination is most important to high-church Anglicans who reject the Roman Catholic teaching that ordained authority is conferred through continued communion with the bishop of Rome. High-church Anglicans replace this understanding with a doctrine proposing an unbroken string of ordinations extending back to the first apostles. As long as a priest has been ordained by the hands of a bishop, who was himself ordained by the hands of another bishop, in a line extending all the way back to Peter himself, the indelible mark has been duly conveyed and the office of priesthood attaches to that individual.

The Form of Government, for example, ordinarily limits the celebration of the Lord's Supper to a teaching elder who has been ordained for that purpose. In situations of pastoral need, however—generally when a teaching elder is unavailable—presbyteries may authorize a ruling elder who has been specially trained and set apart to fulfill that role in a particular church. Apart from certain urgent pastoral-care situations, the decision of when and where the Lord's Supper is celebrated is never made by the individual celebrant but always by a council of the church, most frequently the session (W-2.4012). This is because, in the Reformed tradition, celebration of the sacraments is a function, not a power emanating from a particular office. In the local church, it is the session's responsibility to authorize and prepare for baptism and the Lord's Supper. It is the teaching elder's responsibility to execute the council's mandate.

The Reformed tradition's functional understanding of ordination is explicit in this section: "The basic form of ministry is the ministry of the whole people of God, from whose midst some are called to ordered ministries, to fulfill particular functions. Members and those in ordered ministries serve together under the mandate of Christ" (G-2.0101).

Teaching elders are set apart to fulfill the function of celebrating the sacraments because that is a matter of good order, not because ordination confers upon them any spiritual power beyond that already conferred by the Holy Spirit upon all baptized Christians.

The Privileged Clergy

There is one inappropriate, completely un-Reformed term that still enjoys some currency among Presbyterians—surprisingly so, because it occurs neither in Scripture, nor in any past or present edition of the *Book of Order*. The only place this word occurs in the *Book of Confessions* is in a derogatory Reformation-era reference to the Roman Catholic Church.

The term is "clergy," and it has no place in the Presbyterian Church. The sole exception is certain ecumenical or interfaith conversations, when it can be useful as a neutral category comprising teaching elders, priests, pastors, ministers, rabbis, and imams. In internal Presbyterian discussions, there is no reason for the word ever to be used.

"Clergy" is derived from the Greek word *kleros* (meaning "share" or "portion"), which eventually evolved into the English word "clerk." Although it may not seem a word like "clerk" could convey any exalted privilege, that is true only from the vantage point of contemporary culture. In the pre-Reformation centuries, reading and writing were uncommon skills. Books and other documents were exceedingly rare. "Clerics" effectively monopolized access to Scripture. In smaller communities, they controlled access to legal documents and public proclamations as well. Members of the clergy functioned as gatekeepers, controlling access to all forms of written communication.

The heritage of the word "clergy," therefore, is entirely related to power and privilege. It connotes the sort of unhealthy professionalism that has nothing to do with profession of faith but everything to do with access to exclusive benefits. It is hard to conceive that such a model of ministry is what the church needs to lift up in these post-Christendom days, in a jaded culture crying out for authentic expressions of servant ministry.

Chapter 2

THE MISSION OF THE CHURCH

The Historic Principles—our main focus in this study—are not the only foundational material included in the early chapters. Since 2011, the *Book of Order* has begun with a separate foundational section whose paragraphs are labeled with the F prefix. This section is intended to be foundational not only for the Form of Government but also for the Directory for Worship and the Rules of Discipline. The documents in this F section are arranged not chronologically, but rather according to their content.

The foundational documents come from a variety of sources. Some hail from classic Reformed sources, many centuries old. Others have been imported from earlier editions of the *Book of Order*. Still others are newly written.

The first foundational chapter is called "The Mission of the Church"; the second is "The Church and Its Confessions"; and the third—the one we will spend the most time exploring in this book—is "Principles of Order and Government."

God's Mission

The first section of chapter 1, "God's Mission" (F-1.01), is a brief, reasonably comprehensive theological preface written especially for the 2011–2013 edition of the book. It is an admirably compact expression of the basics of Christian faith according to the Reformed tradition.

While creedal in style, it does not have formal confessional status

---

Unlike amendments to other parts of the *Constitution*, which require approval by a simple majority of General Assembly commissioners, followed by ratification by a simple majority of the presbyteries (G-6.04), amendments to the *Book of Confessions* must go through a more extensive approval process that includes the following steps: (1) approval for study by a simple majority of one General Assembly, (2) revision and recommendation by a special committee of at least fifteen members, (3) approval by a simple majority of a second General Assembly, (4) ratification by a two-thirds majority of the presbyteries, and (5) final approval by simple majority of a third General Assembly (G-6.03).

because it has not undergone the extensive vetting process required of creeds that have become part of the *Book of Confessions*.

Christ the Head of the Church

The next section, "Jesus Christ Is Head of the Church" (F-1.02), was the opening section of the pre-2011 *Book of Order*. It was edited and adapted in minor ways for the present book, but it is substantially the same. A new subsection, "Christ is the Foundation of the Church" (F-1.0205), was added, expressing themes of atonement, reconciliation, and Christ's commission to share good news, which were not explicitly present in the earlier edition.

The Body of Christ

Next comes "The Calling of the Church" (F-1.03), presenting several classic theological expressions of the nature of the church that have long been considered foundational to Reformed ecclesiology.

The first of these is the rich biblical metaphor, from 1 Corinthians 12, of the church as the body of Christ (F-1.0301). This metaphor is here developed into a statement of the church's calling to live as a community of faith, hope, love, and witness. Together, the statements expounding each of these four points form a compact mission statement, worthy of further study by sessions and congregations. It is also suitable for recitation in a creedal fashion in worship.

Particularly noteworthy is the repetition of the word "community." This addresses a common yearning in this highly mobile, fragmented culture, in which people frequently feel alone in a crowd, isolated from their neighbors.

The Classical Marks of the Church

Following this restatement of the biblical image of the church as the body of Christ, the *Constitution* affirms the two sets of marks (or notes) of the church, long treasured by Reformed Christians: the classical marks of unity, holiness, catholicity, and apostolicity, and the Reformed marks of word, sacrament, and discipline.

The classical marks of the church date back at least as far as the Nicene Creed of 381. First is the church's *unity*, which is both a theological reality and an aspirational ideal. For Reformed Christians, the multiplicity of Christian denominations is not so much a cause for lament as a challenge. Denominational divisions may obscure unity, but Presbyterians commit themselves "to the reduction of that obscurity" (F-1.0302a).

Second, the church is meant to be *holy*, although this does not mean Presbyterians fall within the sectarian tradition sometimes labeled "holiness churches." Reformed Christians see holiness as God's gift, not the product of human achievement (F-1.0302b). Although sin is a discouraging and ever-present reality, God calls Christians to rely continually on "the means of grace"—traditionally, word and sacrament, although the Directory for Worship, W-5.5001, adds prayer and worship to this list—as they strive to live a Christlike life.

The *catholicity* of the church—with a small "c," as Presbyterians frequently affirm, to differentiate it from denominations that use the word "Catholic" in their names—witnesses to the truth that, while particular expressions of the church may differ from time to time and from place to place, in essence the church is at all times and everywhere the same church. With this reality in mind, Presbyterians constantly challenge one another "to testify to Christ's embrace of men, women, and children of all times, places, races, nations, ages, conditions, and stations in life" (F-1.0302c).

For Presbyterians, this commitment to radical inclusiveness is no thoughtless affirmation of what some derisively brand "political correctness." Inclusiveness is a spiritual ideal, essential to the disciple's calling. The church catholic—which, because of sin, is always more of an ideal than a reality—looks more integrated in its racial composition, sounds more diverse in its accents, and enjoys at its common meals a greater range of cuisines than any particular congregation we are likely to know in this life.

Finally, the church is *apostolic*. While apostolicity has been variously defined as being in communion with certain bishops or as an unbroken historical string of ordinations dating back to the first apostles, for Presbyterians it is more a matter of action. Apostolicity derives from the truth that God, "by the power of the Spirit . . . sends the Church into the world to share the gospel of God's redemption of all things and people" (F-1.0302d). Apostolic Christians are, quite simply, those who are God-sent.

This compels Presbyterians to pursue an evangelistic mission "to present the claims of Jesus Christ, leading persons to repentance, acceptance of Christ alone as Savior and Lord, and new life as his disciples." Evangelism means more than simply leading others to first-time or renewed Christian commitment. In its fullest sense, evangelism also embodies "worship, prayer, fellowship and service" (F-1.0302d).

The Reformed Marks or "Notes" of the Church

The Reformers, while acknowledging the classical marks' historical and theological importance to the ecumenical church, developed their own distinctive criteria for defining the characteristics of the church of Jesus Christ.

Calvin speaks of just two marks of the church, Word and sacrament. Explaining his theology of ordination, he considers it vital that his two marks of the church be visible in the work of a single person in ordered ministry. This, he believes, is symbolic of the fundamental Reformed principle that sacraments without the Word are but superstition, and the Word without the sacraments is empty.[1]

John Knox moves in a slightly different—but complementary—direction, adding a third mark, discipline:

> The notes of the true Kirk, therefore, we believe, confess, and avow to be: first, the true preaching of the Word of God, in which God has revealed himself to us, as the writings of the prophets and apostles declare; secondly, the right administration of the sacraments of Christ Jesus, with which must be associated the Word and promise of God to seal and confirm them in our hearts; and lastly, ecclesiastical discipline uprightly ministered, as God's Word prescribes, whereby vice is repressed and virtue nourished.[2]

By adding his third mark, or note, of the church, Knox makes it impossible for the order of teaching elder (or, as he called it, minister) to embody the full essence of the church. The first two notes are held in stewardship by those ordained to this role, but the third belongs collectively to the ruling elders (or, as he would call them, simply elders). The church is not the church in the person of a priest performing a private mass, ordained to do so by a bishop. The church is only the church as a corporate body, exercising stewardship of the notes of the church. For Knox, all three marks can never be embodied in one person. Ministers are distinctively stewards of Word and sacrament and elders of ecclesiastical discipline.

The distinctive role of ruling elders is clearly demonstrated in the *Second Book of Discipline*'s description of the duties of the "eldarschip." The eldarschip was the early corporate body in Scotland that was ancestor to both session and presbytery. In this passage in the old Scots dialect, stewardship of all three notes of the kirk is assigned to the eldership, along with the distribution of "ecclesiasticall guidis" (goods), or money. Ordination is the means by which the body of Christ, guided by the Holy Spirit, assigns particular functional tasks to a select portion of its membership. In this way, ordination is bound to the mission of the church. It fulfills a function rather than establishing an office.

---

1. John Calvin, *Institutes of the Christian Religion*, trans. Ford Lewis Battles, ed. John T. McNeill (Louisville, KY: Westminster John Knox Press, 2011), 4.5.10.

2. Scots Confession, chapter 18, in the *Constitution of the Presbyterian Church (U.S.A.)*, Part 1: *Book of Confessions* (Louisville, KY: Office of the General Assembly, 1993).

The Great Ends of the Church

The next foundational document is the Great Ends of the Church (F-1.0304).

The great ends of the Church are:

> the proclamation of the gospel for the salvation of humankind;
> the shelter, nurture, and spiritual fellowship of the children of
>   God;
> the maintenance of divine worship;
> the preservation of the truth;
> the promotion of social righteousness; and
> the exhibition of the Kingdom of Heaven to the world.

The Great Ends first appeared in the *Constitution* of the United Presbyterian Church of North America in 1910. The word "end" here is best understood as "goal," "purpose," or "reason for being." The list is, essentially, a churchwide mission statement.

The Great Ends languished in relative obscurity in modern times, until the moderator of the 208th General Assembly, John Buchanan of the Fourth Presbyterian Church, Chicago, in 1996 proposed a two-year churchwide study of this historic statement of purpose. Buchanan envisioned this as a way of discovering unity, in a time of intense theological disagreement over the ethics of same-sex relationships.

As the church undertook this study, it was discovered that the origins of the Great Ends of the Church had been all but lost to history. Apart from the fact that the statement came into the life of the 1910 General Assembly of the United Presbyterian Church of North America as part of a constitutional revision, no one has been able to discover any further information about its authorship, nor about what circumstances led the church to adopt it.

Buchanan's churchwide study was warmly received by Presbyterians from across the theological spectrum. Chief among its many virtues is that the Great Ends seem to offer something for everyone. From "the proclamation of the gospel for the salvation of humankind" to "the promotion of social righteousness," this historic but still very contemporary mission statement encompasses the entire spectrum of theological opinions and mission priorities.

Openness to the Guidance of the Holy Spirit

Chapter 1 of the Foundations section is rounded out with a collection of brief statements embodying theological principles that have long been valued in the life of the church.

The first of these is a statement on Continuity and Change, which—without mentioning it specifically—echoes another saying of uncertain origin, the well-known Latin proverb, *Ecclesia reformata semper reformanda secundum verbum Dei.* Some translate this as "The reformed church, always reforming according to the Word of God," while others insist on the more literal but less poetic "The church reformed, always to be reformed according to the Word of God"—which, in fact, is the translation given in F-2.02.

When this section points out that "[a]s the Church seeks reform and fresh direction, it looks to Jesus Christ who goes ahead of us and calls us to follow him," it truly reflects the spirit of *Ecclesia reformata semper reformanda* (F-1.0401). The accent here is on the dynamic nature of the Holy Spirit's interaction with the church and on the necessity of the church's remaining ever ready to move in new directions in response to the Spirit's leading.

Next comes a brief but extremely far-reaching statement on Ecumenicity: "The presbyterian system of government in the Constitution of the Presbyterian Church (U.S.A.) is established in light of Scripture but is not regarded as essential for the existence of the Christian Church nor required of all Christians" (F-1.0402).

This single sentence is remarkable for its theological humility and for the ways it differs from many Presbyterian theological statements of earlier centuries.

The next item, Unity in Diversity, begins by citing the famous teaching of Paul from Galatians 3:28, that in Christ "[t]here is no longer Jew or Greek, there is no longer slave or free, there is no longer male and female; for all of you are one in Christ Jesus." Building on that scriptural foundation, it is a natural next step to declare that "there is . . . no place in the life of the Church for discrimination against any person" (F-1.0403).

The last of these miscellaneous foundational documents, Openness, carries this theme of radical inclusiveness even further (F-1.0404). Exhorting the church to openness in a variety of dimensions, this section concludes chapter 1 with a rhetorical flourish.

Chapter 3

THE CHURCH AND ITS CONFESSIONS

Status Confessionis

We have seen how confessional statements in the Reformed tradition occupy a tertiary layer of authority, below Jesus Christ as head of the church and below the Scriptures. The section on The Church and Its Confessions begins by listing some of the functions confessions of faith fulfill in the church: "They guide the church in its study and interpretation of the Scriptures; they summarize the essence of Reformed Christian tradition; they direct the church in maintaining sound doctrines; they equip the church for its work of proclamation. They serve to strengthen personal commitment and the life and witness of the community of believers" (F-2.01).

The next observation, that the Confessions "arose in response to particular circumstances within the history of God's people" and "claim the truth of the Gospel at those points where their authors perceived that truth to be at risk" refers to a situation known in theological terms as a *status confessionis.*

The church does not restate its faith in confessional form merely because a number of years have elapsed since it issued its last confession. The assumption is that there must be some pressing reason for stating the essentials of the faith anew—usually some controversy that is begging for an authoritative restatement of what Jesus Christ is saying to the church and to the world.

In the case of most Presbyterian confessions, the answer to the question "What is the *status confessionis?*" is clear. In the case of the Nicene Creed, the church had a pressing need to settle christological controversies that were threatening to tear it apart. The Reformation-era confessions—the Scots Confession, the Heidelberg Catechism, the Second Helvetic Confession, and the Westminster Confession and Catechisms—were written at various times, for various nations and language groups, during the religious wars of the sixteenth century. The Theological Declaration of Barmen gave voice to the Confessing Church in Nazi Germany as it resisted its totalitarian rulers' efforts to suppress its prophetic voice. The Confession of 1967 allowed the United Presbyterian Church in the U.S.A. to speak a message both prophetic and reassuring to a nation deeply divided over war and racism.

With respect to the Confession of Belhar—the declaration of faith issued by the "colored" Reformed church in South Africa during the apartheid era—there is little question that this creed spoke deep truth, in its day, to a sharply divided church. Many American Presbyterians believe that, like the Theological Declaration of Barmen, the Belhar Confession continues to speak prophetically today, to a church in a very different cultural context that continues to struggle against racism.

For the remaining confessions, the nature of the *status confessionis* is less readily apparent. In the case of the Apostles' Creed, the question is difficult to answer, because we simply know so little about the creed's origins. We know it was used in western Europe from a very early era as a baptismal formula, to catechize adults coming to Christian faith for the first time, but apart from that, it is impossible to speak of its source.

With respect to the Brief Statement of Faith (1990), we know the confession came about because the General Assembly saw the need for a brief expression of the Reformed faith in modern language, suitable for use as a creed by God's people in worship. The effort did not arise out of any particular controversy.

Subordinate Standards

We have already seen how the Confession of 1967 defines the Confessions as "subordinate standards" (9.03). To call a confession of faith a subordinate standard is in no way to demean its importance to the church. The adjective merely points out that there are higher authorities: the Scriptures and Jesus Christ, the head of the church.

In the words of the *Book of Order*, the Confessions "are not lightly drawn up or subscribed to, nor may they be ignored or dismissed. The church is prepared to instruct, counsel with, or even to discipline one ordained who seriously rejects the faith expressed in the confessions" (F-2.02).

The church continues to wrestle with the question of precisely how the Confessions serve as standards, when strict subscriptionism (see text box) is a thing of the past. It is worthwhile to examine several different ways the word "standard" is commonly used, to arrive at a more nuanced understanding.

Excavating the most venerable of ancient cities, archaeologists have come upon stone or cast-metal objects that functioned as measuring standards for weighing out agricultural produce. The prophet Amos rails against those who "make the ephah small and the shekel great, and practice deceit with false balances" (Amos 8:5). Subscriptionists value the Confessions as immutable points of comparison in just that way.

But that is not the only meaning of "standard." The word also describes

For centuries, Presbyterian churches practiced "subscriptionism"—the requirement that teaching elders accept the Westminster Confession in its entirety as "the system of doctrine contained in the scriptures." This practice persisted well into the twentieth century. Early in that century, Presbyterians took the remarkable step of amending that sixteenth-century confession in order to make it consistent with modern sensibilities. In 1903, the Presbyterian Church, U.S.A. added chapters on the Holy Spirit and Missions and softened double predestination. In 1958 that same denomination added a statement on Marriage and Divorce—an action echoed by the Presbyterian Church, U.S. in 1981. Not until the Confession of 1967 brought in the concept of a *Book of Confessions*—acknowledging that all confessions are, to some degree, creatures of their own historical era—did the last vestige of a subscriptionist understanding disappear.

certain jazz melodies that serve as frequent starting points for improvisation. Aspiring jazz musicians are expected to learn the standards, a corpus of timeless tunes they will spend the rest of their careers playfully adapting. Though undergoing many and varied alterations, the tunes remain recognizably themselves.

Sometimes it can be difficult to determine precisely where a jazz standard ends and where improvisation begins. No analysis of individual notes, no matter how meticulous, can reveal that borderline. The standard is undoubtedly present, but in jazz its edges are indistinct, its essence malleable.

The same is true of how confessions function in the present-day church. There is no absolute purity of doctrine in these documents. These impassioned statements were written amid the sound and fury of controversy. They contain time-bound elements alongside eternal truths. We can understand each confession, in its own era, as a fresh improvisation. When we study them all together and note their historical particularities, a composite picture emerges that is inspired by the original but not rigidly bound to it.

A third meaning of "standard" is the flag soldiers carried into battle in earlier centuries. Such banners served a purpose both inspirational and practical. In the smoky chaos of nineteenth-century warfare, soldiers all up and down the line of attack could look to the battle standard and see that their side's advance had not been turned back, that there was still hope of winning the day. If the soldier holding the flag happened to fall, a comrade would swoop in and lift the banner high once again, despite the personal risk. The battle standard was an essential means of communication. Hundreds of others were looking to that flag, eager for reassurance.

In times of spiritual turmoil, confessions serve as tangible signs that, in the words of the Brief Statement of Faith,

> Like mother who will not forsake her nursing child,
> like a father who welcomes the prodigal home,
> God is faithful still. (10.3)

This is not to say confessional standards are unchanging. There is a dynamic quality to the church's ongoing confessional activity. In the words of the Confession of 1967, "In every age, the church has expressed its witness in words and deeds as the needs of the time required. . . . No one type of confession is exclusively valid, no one statement is irreformable. Obedience to Jesus Christ alone identifies the one universal church and supplies the continuity of its tradition" (9.03).

The Smithsonian Institution in Washington, DC, proudly displays the battle standard that inspired the US national anthem. The oversized Star-Spangled Banner now on display flew over Baltimore's Fort McHenry the day after the battle, giving hope to Francis Scott Key. Although thousands of visitors stroll by it every day, its appearance is hardly attractive. Its blues and reds are faded, its whites are yellowed, and gaping holes are visible. The quality of the fabric is so frail that, were the banner to be removed from its protective glass and run up a flagpole, it would surely fall apart. Spangled with stars it may be, but their number is far fewer than today's full complement of fifty.

Yet no one is looking to see that historic flag catch a breeze again. It is not its several yards of fabric that hold such significance for museum-goers but the intangible values it represents. It has been reproduced millions of times since, flying over battlefields that Francis Scott Key could never have imagined. The Iwo Jima flag is its direct descendant. So too is the banner rescue workers flew from a twisted girder of New York's ruined World Trade Center after 9/11.

There are portions of some historic confessions that have clearly outlived their usefulness. The presence of such passages in the *Book of Confessions* is akin to the place of the Star-Spangled Banner in the Smithsonian. They still have a vital role to play in inspiring God's people, just not in the active sense. There now fly from the parapets newer standards that recall the confessions of ages past but are not identical to them.

To say this is in no way to diminish these historic standards' importance in the life of the church. They have their place, and it remains an honored one. Some people cannot perceive how frail they have become and have become so attached to the original piece of cloth that they would burglarize the museum in the middle of the night and bear the flag into battle again. They ultimately betray the ideals for which these proud confessions stand.

Timeless Truths and Cultural Intrusions

Two confessions, the Apostles' Creed and the Nicene Creed, bear witness to "the faith of the church catholic." These express timeless truths of "the mystery of the triune God and of the incarnation of the eternal Word of God in Jesus Christ" (F-2.03). As such, they are treasured symbols of unity for all Christians.

Other creeds embody the spirit of the Protestant Reformation. "God's grace in Jesus Christ as revealed in the Scriptures" is at the heart of their proclamation, as well as "the Protestant watchwords—grace alone, faith alone, Scripture alone" (F-2.04).

So, what in these centuries-old confessions is the timeless essence, the iconic words that continue to speak afresh to believers of every age? What is the dross that can be discarded as time-bound and irrelevant to contemporary need? To answer that question is difficult. On numerous occasions in recent years, presbyteries have overtured the General Assembly to come up with a list of "essential tenets of the Reformed faith," so as to inform ordained leaders what their promise to "receive and adopt" the Confessions really means (W-4.4003c). The Assembly has consistently refused to produce such a list, leaving it up to ordaining councils (presbyteries in the case of teaching elders, and sessions in the case of ruling elders and deacons) to decide what is essential.

This is not to say that every Reformation ideal deserves to be carried forward into the present day. Parts of the Reformation-era confessions are clearly outdated. Among these are the Scots Confession's teaching that absolute obedience is owed to kings and other rulers as God's agents on earth (3.24); the Heidelberg Catechism's branding the Roman Catholic mass as "a condemnable idolatry" (4.080); the Second Helvetic Confession's condemnation of monks as being "of no use to the church of God" and "pernicious" (5.149), as well as its ban on women performing baptisms (5.191); the Westminster Confession's naming of the pope "usurper of Christ" (6.145); and the Westminster Larger Catechism's enthusiastic support of a rigid class system by which some people are "superiors" and others "inferiors" by birth (7.234–7.242). Twenty-first-century Christians studying the Reformation-era confessions must be prepared to be awed by profoundly beautiful teachings one minute and appalled by prejudicial, culture-bound assumptions in the next.

The closest thing in the *Book of Order* to a list of essential tenets is the following list of themes central to the Reformed tradition: "the majesty, holiness, and providence of God who in Christ and by the power of the Spirit creates, sustains, rules, and redeems the world in the freedom of sovereign righteousness and love." Related to this central affirmation of God's sovereignty are other great themes of the Reformed tradition:

The election of the people of God for service as well as for salvation;

Covenant life marked by a disciplined concern for order in the church according to the Word of God;

A faithful stewardship that shuns ostentation and seeks proper use of the gifts of God's creation; and

The recognition of the human tendency to idolatry and tyranny, which calls the people of God to work for the transformation of society by seeking justice and living in obedience to the Word of God. (F-2.05)

The Confessions of the church—even the most ancient—are living documents. We honor them best when we treat them not as hallowed artifacts but rather as the subject of respectful debate and dialogue, as together we seek to discern Christ's will for the church.

Chapter 4

THE HISTORIC PRINCIPLES AND THE COLONIAL EXPERIENCE

The year was 1785. Under the ill-considered Articles of Confederation, the thirteen states were struggling through their first, failing experiment in federal government. In just two years' time, delegates to a national convention would vote to send the US Constitution out to state legislatures for ratification.

Among Presbyterians, similar efforts were under way to provide ecclesiastical governance on the national level. Although only Presbyterians from northern states were involved at this stage, as the Synod of New York and Philadelphia appointed ten ministers to develop a constitutional document, they were on their way to forming a truly national church.

The synod gave its committee the following commission:

> [To] take into consideration, the Constitution of the Church of Scotland, & other Protestant Churches; & agreeably to the general principles of Presbyterian Government, to compile a system of general rules for the Government of the Synod & the several Presbyteries under their inspection; & the people in their communion. & to make a report of their proceeding at the next meeting of Synod.[1]

European Roots

What these American Presbyterians were doing was unprecedented. Never before had a Reformed church body, under presbyterian governance, formed itself by building upwards from the grassroots level. Until that time, Reformed churches had been established from the top down, often after a period of armed conflict. They came into being through a process of reforming existing church structures, under the oversight and protection of sympathetic civil authorities. The founders of the Reformed tradition believed the approbation of these secular rulers was essential to establishing national church order along presbyterian lines.

This had been true in John Calvin's Geneva. In the Swiss canton system, principal cities were the highest level of government, and Calvin's political fortunes waxed and waned in proportion to the amount of backing he

---

1. Guy S. Klett, ed., *Minutes of the Presbyterian Church in America, 1706–1788* (Philadelphia: Presbyterian Historical Society, 1976), 597.

obtained from city authorities. For a time Calvin was exiled to Strasbourg, as opposition forces sought to turn back the momentum of his reforms. When the political pendulum swung back again, presbyterian church government became permanently established, and Calvin himself assumed a dominant role in secular as well as ecclesiastical government.

The same was true in the British Isles, where Calvinists in England and Scotland mounted their own separate campaigns to convince the crown to establish presbyterian church order.

In the Church of England, the Puritan party's burgeoning strength led to nearly a century of bloody religious warfare. The presbyterian high-water mark was achieved under the rule of the Lord Protector, Oliver Cromwell. A king in all but name, the Puritan leader Cromwell was a brutal but effective ruler. After his death—and a brief, doomed effort to replace him with his ineffectual son, Richard—Parliament turned to the Anglican-leaning Charles II, son of the deposed Charles I. The restoration of the English monarchy meant that Calvinist church order would never again prevail in England—although a notable Puritan minority faction would persist within the Church of England, evolving eventually into the "low church" wing of Anglicanism. Some congregationalists would continue as well, pursuing a tenuous existence under the label "nonconformist."

Likewise, in Scotland, no one questioned the assumption that it would take more than winning the hearts of individual believers to reform the church. The turbulent relationship between John Knox and his Roman Catholic sovereign, Mary Queen of Scots, was a political struggle that paralleled the ecclesiastical reform. It took a cadre of scheming Protestant nobles to depose the queen and pave the way for real ecclesiastical change. For more than a century following the establishment of the presbyterian Church of Scotland as the national church, warfare continued between Catholic and Protestant factions. Few questioned the assumption that the game of establishing a new church had to be winner-take-all.

This was because both contending theological camps—Roman Catholic as well as Protestant—held what was essentially the same political philosophy. The divine right of kings was a given. Both believed that, in the ideal government, church and state were seamlessly linked. Both sides took it for granted that those who found themselves on the losing side of the wars of reformation would be relegated to ineffectual minority status, and could stand to lose their churches, property, and sometimes even their lives.

Reinventing the Church in a New World

During these centuries of ecclesiastical struggle, small but significant numbers of refugees fled the melee of the wars of religion, making the arduous voyage across the Atlantic to the New World. In Puritan New England, the founders of both the Plymouth and Massachusetts Bay colonies sought to establish the same sort of godly commonwealth they had yearned to see take root in the soil of their native England. There was effectively no separation between church and state in the early New England colonies—as dissenters like Roger Williams, Anne Hutchinson, and the Quaker martyr Mary Dyer discovered to their dismay. The elders of the Massachusetts Bay colony considered it an act of mercy to allow Williams and his followers to settle the tiny tract of Rhode Island, treating it as a sort of ecclesiastical leper colony.

The situation was different in the Middle Atlantic colonies. In the melting pot of New York, where Dutch merchants and mariners rubbed elbows with all manner of new arrivals, churches of various descriptions achieved an uneasy but peaceful coexistence. Far removed from church oversight structures back in their mother countries, these congregations adopted a practical congregationalism at first, even if it was not their theological ideal. In New Jersey, Scots and Scots-Irish immigrants were the most numerous group, tolerated by the Anglican-sympathizing Colonial governors but never able to achieve established status. The Quaker William Penn had founded his colony of Pennsylvania by royal charter, explicitly as a haven for dissenters from various religious groups. In Maryland, the Calvert family provided a similar refuge for Roman Catholics, but—mindful of the tenuous status of their coreligionists back home—they were broadly tolerant of other religious groups as well.

In the South, pockets of Scots and Scots-Irish Presbyterians established their own ecclesiastical and community life, while maintaining an uneasy relationship with the Anglican Colonial authorities. Periodically, they fought legal battles over the question of whether their taxes should be used to build and maintain Anglican churches.

While many histories of the Presbyterian Church (U.S.A.) begin with the adoption of the first Form of Government, it is a mistake to neglect the century and a half of Colonial church life that preceded it. The pieces of that historic document would never have fallen into place as they did without the heritage of effective congregationalism arising from the isolation of Colonial churches, colored by the living memory of Reformation-era religious persecution that had made parts of Europe into killing fields.

A Voice of Toleration Crying in the Wilderness

One other British development is especially worthy of mention. A highlight of the Glorious Revolution that placed William and Mary of the Netherlands on the British throne was Parliament's 1689 passage of the Act of Toleration. This unprecedented edict extended to dissenting Protestants a measure of civil recognition. While continuing the episcopal Church of England as the established church in that country and the presbyterian Church of Scotland as such north of the border, minority groups were for the first time officially permitted to carry on their church life unmolested, as long as they swore allegiance to the crown. Roman Catholics and non-Trinitarians were explicitly excluded from the arrangement, but English Reformed Christians saw something new appearing in their midst: a non-established but officially tolerated church.

The ripples of this change radiated outward, lapping up against the western shores of the Atlantic. Jailed by the Anglican-sympathizing governor of New York for "preaching without a license," the Presbyterian evangelist Francis Makemie successfully challenged his arrest in court on the grounds that it violated the Act of Toleration.

As Makemie's theological descendants endured the turmoil of the Revolutionary War—and, following that, a decade or so of civil difficulties under the Articles of Confederation—they became convinced that the Presbyterian church in the new nation would have to be structured differently from its European counterparts. Theirs would be a new church for this brave New World, with all thoughts of establishing a state-supported national church set aside.

Even so, for them toleration had its limits—as we will see in our discussion of the first Historic Principle, "God alone is Lord of the conscience." "Toleration" meant freedom from governmental persecution of religious minorities and was in no way meant to suggest that the church could not define the boundaries of its own understanding of orthodoxy.

It is impossible to understand the 1788 Historic Principles of Church Order (F-3.01) without seeing them as an expression of the Colonial experience. Except, perhaps, for their archaic vocabulary, this cultural gap is the single greatest obstacle to understanding for those who read these eighteenth-century words today. Without recalling the historical context of centuries of religious struggle that were still a living memory for the document's drafters, twenty-first-century readers can hardly help but see the language of the Historic Principles as dense, impenetrable, and of little relevance to the present day. Understood in their historical context, however, these foundational principles come to life in unexpected ways—as we will soon see in the second part of this study.

PART II
PRINCIPLES

Chapter 5

GOD IS LORD
OF THE CONSCIENCE

a. God alone is Lord of the conscience, and hath left it free from the doctrines and commandments of men which are in anything contrary to his Word, or beside it, in matters of faith or worship.

b. Therefore we consider the rights of private judgment, in all matters that respect religion, as universal and unalienable: We do not even wish to see any religious constitution aided by the civil power, further than may be necessary for protection and security, and at the same time, be equal and common to all others. (F-3.0101)

The declaration "God alone is Lord of the conscience" is the most widely misunderstood of the Historic Principles of Church Order. A great many modern readers lift the first seven words out of context, failing to attend to the remainder of the sentence or to the further explanation that follows in the second paragraph. Consequently, they fail to understand how this principle functioned in its eighteenth-century setting.

The initial impulse, from the twenty-first-century standpoint, is to treat the first seven words as a sort of bumper-sticker slogan promoting unfettered, freethinking morality. But this is not its purpose at all. Were it so, there would be little difference between "God alone is Lord of the conscience" and the lament of Judges 17:6 that "all the people did what was right in their own eyes."

The Westminster Context: Free Choice within Limits

The first part of this Historic Principle is a verbatim quotation from the Westminster Confession. There is an important qualifier here: "which are in anything contrary to his Word, or beside it." With respect to matters of faith or worship, God frees the conscience from becoming entangled in anything that has no basis in the Bible. Far from being a freethinker's manifesto, the first seven words affirm that human conscience is captive to the Word of God.

This is clearly evident if we trace that one-sentence quotation from the Westminster Confession back to its original source. Here is the full paragraph, which would have been well known to the Colonial divines who penned the first Form of Government:

> God alone is Lord of the conscience, and hath left it free from the doc-
> trines and commandments of men which are in anything contrary to
> his Word, or beside it, in matters of faith or worship. So that to believe
> such doctrines, or to obey such commandments out of conscience,
> is to betray true liberty of conscience; and the requiring an implicit
> faith, and an absolute and blind obedience, is to destroy liberty of
> conscience, and reason also. (6.109)

The point that is so difficult to comprehend in the present day is that early American Presbyterians believed conscience is actually freer when it operates within the limits of divine guidance than would be the case if it roamed about completely unfettered. Such is not the contemporary under-standing of freedom. The authors of the Historic Principles are saying that, when Christians carefully attend to the teachings of Scripture, they are freed from the dreadful consequences of being wrong. To their thinking, freedom is less about choice and more about choosing rightly.

Christian conscience, according to Westminster, is free—but only from constraint by moral authorities whose teachings contradict God's Word in Scripture. If the Scriptures command a certain behavior as moral or con-demn its opposite as immoral, there is no question in their minds but that the Christian must unhesitatingly obey.

Paradoxically, it is in strict obedience to God's law that true freedom is found. In the opening section of this twentieth chapter, "Of Christian Liberty, and Liberty of Conscience," the Westminster Confession defines what it means by freedom:

> The liberty which Christ hath purchased for believers under the gos-
> pel consists in their freedom from the guilt of sin, the condemning
> wrath of God, the curse of the moral law, and in their being delivered
> from this present evil world, bondage to Satan, and dominion of sin,
> from the evil of afflictions, the sting of death, the victory of the grave,
> and everlasting damnation; and also in their free access to God, and
> their yielding obedience unto him, not out of slavish fear, but a child-
> like love and a willing mind.

Christian liberty, in other words, is not a matter of being "free for." It is a matter of being "free from"—free from the horrible consequences of sin. Christian freedom is found in "yielding obedience" to God, out of "child-like love and a willing mind."

Christians who wholeheartedly commit their hearts to the Lord of the conscience and who strive to live a virtuous life discover how their Lord

Imagine that a Christian is placed on an elevated road, with steep precipices to either side. To the rear is a ravenous beast, blocking any backward progress. God says to the Christian, "You are free." That freedom consists not in the ability to turn right nor left, nor to turn around and proceed in the opposite direction—a freedom the Christian does theoretically have, although the consequences of choosing any direction but one would be disastrous. What God means in saying, "You are free"—according to the Westminster divines—is that Christians are freed from the depredations of the beast. Only one choice is the right one; all others lead to catastrophe: so why ask the question? The only freedom of conscience that matters is freedom to choose God's way.

Some may, in fact, choose differently: believing they can either prevail against the ravenous beast or discover handholds on the sheer face of the precipice to ease themselves down safely. Woe to them, say these early Presbyterians! Only the faithful believer who unquestioningly chooses the high road to liberty, graciously constructed by Christ through his saving death on the cross, is truly free in the end.

blesses them in the here and now, through the inner light of their own consciences. They find they are able to sleep at night.

Private vs. Public Judgment

So why should the framers of the Historic Principles give freedom of conscience such a prominent place, if there really is no question as to which option Christians must choose? The answer is apparent only in the second paragraph of this principle.

They are speaking, in this second part, about "the rights of private judgment, in all matters that respect religion." Conscience, to them, is the internal decision-making process whereby Christians choose the one truly sensible choice that is available to them: the way of Christ. The specific reason why this concerns them is embodied in numerous stories they could all recount, based on their ancestors' experiences: stories of a politically established national church that sought to exercise tyrannical control over the private beliefs of an entire populace.

The constraint of conscience this Historic Principle opposes is no casual difference of opinion. It is persecution, by the party holding political power, of those professing dissenting beliefs.

Perhaps the writers of the Historic Principles were thinking of Roger Williams and Anne Hutchinson, exiled by the civil government of the Massachusetts Bay colony on account of the free exercise of their conscience. Or maybe they were recalling Mary Dyer, who in that same colony was executed by hanging on account of her Quaker convictions. Or perhaps it was the memory of any one of a number of English or Scottish martyrs who had seen homes and fortunes confiscated by the crown, and in some cases even sacrificed their lives.

Orthodoxy Still Has Its Boundaries

The fact that these same writers also produced the second Historic Principle—declaring that "every Christian Church . . . is entitled to declare the terms of admission into its communion"—demonstrates that freedom of conscience in no way undermines the right of churches to draw boundaries around their own systems of belief and declare that particular individuals are either inside or outside those boundaries. In other words, "God alone is Lord of the conscience" has to do not so much with the right to persist in dissent within a church but rather to do so *outside* it.

"We do not even wish to see any religious constitution *aided* by the civil power," continues the second part of the first Historic Principle. Its authors want to distance themselves even from the sort of arrangement that prevailed in England and Scotland following the 1689 Act of Toleration: one church established as the national church ("aided by the civil power," in other words) and others being merely tolerated. Civil authorities need to stay out of the realm of religious conscience altogether, for, in the kingdom of conscience, only God is Lord. Today we would refer to this second Historic Principle as an early formulation of the separation of church and state.

This sounds commonplace to Americans today, after more than two centuries of living under the First Amendment to the US Constitution, but in the late eighteenth century it was a radical stance. Not so many years after the General Assembly adopted this first Historic Principle, the First Amendment to the US Constitution was ratified. The fact that the church chose to incorporate a similar conviction into its own *Constitution*, even before the civil authorities made it the law of the land, demonstrates how Presbyterians were leading the way for the entire nation.

"Before I can live with other folks I've got to live with myself. The one thing that doesn't abide by majority rule is a person's conscience."

—Atticus Finch to his daughter, Scout, in Harper Lee's novel, *To Kill a Mockingbird*

Conscience in the *Book of Order*

The Presbyterian Church (U.S.A.) continues to honor individual conscience. In G-1.0302, "Welcome and Openness," the Form of Government declares: "A congregation shall welcome all persons who trust in God's grace in Jesus Christ and desire to become part of the fellowship and ministry of his Church" (F-1.0403). No person shall be denied membership for any reason not related to profession of faith.

The nature of this profession of faith is made clear in G-1.0301, which describes a covenant of membership that commences with "profession of faith in Jesus Christ as Lord and Savior." In the case of those not already baptized, that sacrament is celebrated immediately after this profession of faith takes place (W-2.3012c).

Those asking to become members of Presbyterian churches frequently want to know what sort of public profession of faith they will be expected to make. Some may have prior experience with independent churches who prominently display a detailed statement of doctrine on their Web page, expecting church members to subscribe to every point. The Presbyterian Church (U.S.A.) has a *Book of Confessions* of nearly three hundred pages but demands its members affirm almost none of it—not even the Apostles' Creed. Although a pastor may well use excerpts from the *Book of Confessions* as a teaching tool in new-member classes, when it comes time for those new members to be publicly received in a service of worship, the only profession of faith they are asked to make is that Jesus Christ is their Lord and Savior.

Why is this, for a denomination like the Presbyterians, who have such a proud tradition of nurturing the life of the mind? Partly it arises out of a truly evangelical conviction—in the classic and oldest meaning of "evangelical"—that the church needs to meet people where they are and welcome them as who they are. There will be time, later, to invite them into deeper engagement with Christian doctrine, as they hear the Word proclaimed and receive the sacraments over many seasons.

When it comes to the church's ordained leadership, there is a different requirement. Those ordained as teaching elders, ruling elders, or deacons are required to answer the ordination questions of W-4.4003

> The essential Christian confession is, as the first answer of the Heidelberg Catechism attests, "That I am not my own, but belong—body and soul, in life and in death—to my faithful savior, Jesus Christ" (4.001). Such a commitment is sufficient. All else that is necessary will follow in due course.

affirmatively. Imbedded in these vows are some declarations of conscience, of the doctrinal variety, that go beyond a simple profession of faith in Christ. They include an acknowledgment of Christ's authority as head of the church as well as belief in the Trinity: *"Do you trust in Jesus Christ your Savior, acknowledge him Lord of all and Head of the Church, and through him believe in one God, Father, Son, and Holy Spirit?"* They require acceptance of the Bible as authoritative in a personal sense: *"Do you accept the Scriptures of the Old and New Testaments to be, by the Holy Spirit, the unique and authoritative witness to Jesus Christ in the Church universal, and God's Word to you?"*

The vows call ordained leaders to deepen their relationship with the *Book of Confessions*, placing themselves under the tutelage of saints from generations past and seeking to discern in their ancient witness the "essential tenets" of the faith: *"Do you sincerely receive and adopt the essential tenets of the Reformed faith as expressed in the confessions of our church as authentic and reliable expositions of what Scripture leads us to believe and do, and will you be instructed and led by those confessions as you lead the people of God? Will you fulfill your ministry in obedience to Jesus Christ, under the authority of Scripture, and be continually guided by our confessions?"*

These promises require ordained leaders to pay close attention to the *Book of Order* as well, heeding its instruction with such diligence that true friendship with their colleagues in ministry will ensue: *"Will you be governed by our church's polity, and will you abide by its discipline? Will you be a friend among your colleagues in ministry, working with them, subject to the ordering of God's Word and Spirit?"*

Ordained leaders promise not to limit their discipleship to the space within the four walls of the church but to see their ordination as a spiritual blessing overflowing into their everyday lives. As this occurs, the fruits of their relationship with Christ become apparent to others. They promise to live publicly as people of conscience, so their lives become a positive example to others and ultimately sow peace, unity, and purity in the church as well: *"Will you in your own life seek to follow the Lord Jesus Christ, love your neighbors, and work for the reconciliation of the world? Do you promise to further the peace, unity, and purity of the church? Will you pray for and seek to serve the people with energy, intelligence, imagination, and love?"*

The several questions that follow are specific to each order of ministry, but they all conclude with the same promise: *"In your ministry will you try to show the love and justice of Jesus Christ?"* This, again, affirms that an actively engaged Christian conscience—far from being a private, interior matter—publicly bears witness to the faith within.

As we read in the Scriptures, "You will know them by their fruits" (Matt. 7:16).

The Bounds of Conscience

Section G2.0105, "Freedom of Conscience," reaffirms that those who serve in ordered ministries "shall adhere to the essentials of the Reformed faith and polity." It allows for a certain freedom of conscience with respect to the interpretation of Scripture but is quick to point out that there are limits to this freedom:

> It is to be recognized, however, that in entering the ordered ministries of the Presbyterian Church (U.S.A.), one chooses to exercise freedom of conscience within certain bounds. His or her conscience is captive to the Word of God as interpreted in the standards of the church so long as he or she continues to seek, or serve in, ordered ministry. The decision as to whether a person has departed from essentials of Reformed faith and polity is made initially by the individual concerned but ultimately becomes the responsibility of the council in which he or she is a member.

Sessions exercise this oversight in the case of ruling elders and deacons, and presbyteries in the case of teaching elders.

In 1962, the Rev. Maurice McCrackin of Cincinnati, Ohio, was tried by the Permanent Judicial Commission of the United Presbyterian Church in the U.S.A. He had appealed an earlier action by the Presbytery of Cincinnati to remove his ordination. The charge was that, as an act of civil disobedience, he had for several years refused to pay his taxes to the United States government.

McCrackin had withheld his taxes as a position of conscience, based on his own pacifist conviction that government involvement in war is immoral. His defense before the Permanent Judicial Commission was that, because his was a position of conscience, and God alone is Lord of the conscience, the church should honor his personal convictions and not take any disciplinary action against him. The Permanent Judicial Commission disagreed, removing McCrackin from ordained ministry.

After a lifetime of outspoken political activism and numerous civil-disobedience arrests, the elderly McCrackin learned in 1987 that friends had convinced the Presbytery of Baltimore to overture the General Assembly to restore his ordination. The Assembly, declaring its desire "to wipe this error off the slate of the church," not only restored McCrackin's ordination but publicly apologized and asked his forgiveness for the action its predecessor Assembly had taken. It was a sign that the conscience of the church had changed on the question of civil disobedience.

Presbyterian government charges those in ordered ministry, in following their consciences, to do so in ways that do not undermine the right of councils to express their own consciences collectively. The *Book of Order* includes a significant footnote to G-2.0105, quoting a 1758 excerpt from the plan of reunion of the Synod of New York and Philadelphia that marked the end of the Old Side/New Side split:

> That when any matter is determined by a majority vote, every member shall either actively concur with or passively submit to such determination; or if his conscience permit him to do neither, he shall, after sufficient liberty modestly to reason and remonstrate, peaceably withdraw from our communion without attempting to make any schism. Provided always that this shall be understood to extend only to such determination as the body shall judge indispensable in doctrine or Presbyterian government. (Plan of Union of 1758, par. 2, in Hist. Dig. (P), 1310)

This instruction gives voice to an important rule of decorum that all members of councils do well to bear in mind whenever they find themselves on the minority side of a vote. In the course of parliamentary debate, they have every right—indeed, every encouragement—vigorously to voice their opinions. But once the vote is taken, if they find they cannot actively support the decision of the majority, ordinarily their responsibility is to "passively submit" (there are exceptions for the special cases of dissents and protests; see below).

Few actions are more destructive in the life of a community than leaders with a minority viewpoint who vociferously complain about a vote that did not go their way. Theologically, Presbyterians believe the Holy Spirit is active in the governance process. For that reason, it is incumbent on all council members humbly to seek to discern the Spirit's direction in the outcome of votes taken. This is not to say it never happens that "councils may err," but it does suggest that outspoken expressions of conscience from those on the losing side of votes ought to be exceedingly rare.

Pastoral Confidentiality

Typically, in situations of pastoral care, conscience requires the counselor not to divulge details shared by an individual in a counseling session. This privilege derives from the long-standing legal principle of the sacredness or "seal" of the confessional, by which priests from denominations with a tradition of sacramental confession are protected from having to reveal the contents of such private conversations.

While there is not a precise correspondence between the sacramental duties of a Roman Catholic priest in the confessional booth and the nonsacramental setting of a Presbyterian teaching elder conversing with a counselee in the study, there is considerable secular case law that considers such conversations equally privileged. Those seeking a precise determination should consult an attorney who is familiar with the laws of their particular state. That case law may not extend to situations in which there is more than one person present besides the teaching elder; if a third party is present, the conversation may not be legally protected, and in some jurisdictions may be subject to subpoena in a court of law.

The *Book of Order* provides further parameters for such privileged conversations. It encourages pastoral counselors to "hold in confidence all information revealed to them" in the course of rendering pastoral care, except for situations in which the counselee has expressly waived the right to privacy (G-4.0301). There is an exception to this ordinary understanding of privacy in counseling relationships: counselors generally have the right to break confidence if they believe there is risk of imminent bodily harm to any person.

Going further, this section on "Confidence and Privilege" mandates reporting to "ecclesiastical and civil authorities"—including police and other law enforcement officials—in certain specialized cases. These are cases involving "harm, or the risk of harm, related to the physical abuse, neglect, and/or sexual molestation or abuse of a minor or an adult who lacks mental capacity." If such information has been shared with the teaching elder in the course of a nonprivileged conversation, there is no question but that he or she must report it. Even in the case of a privileged conversation, if the counselor "reasonably believes that there is risk of future physical harm or abuse," it has ceased to be a matter of professional discretion: the counselor is absolutely required to report it (G-4.0302).

Dissents and Protests

Another practical way in which the right of conscience is preserved in the *Book of Order* is its provisions for dissents and protests. Although these provisions are not as frequently used as they could be, they provide important protections.

If, during debate, it becomes apparent to a member of a council that the body is taking a position that is an affront to his or her conscience, the member is not required simply to endure the experience silently. The person can file a dissent, "expressing disagreement with a decision of a council," or a protest, "alleging that a decision of a council is or contains an irregularity or a delinquency" (G-3.0105).

While it is necessary to act quickly to file a dissent or protest—these documents can be accepted only before adjournment—councils are required not only to receive dissents and protests without question or debate but also to preserve them in their minutes.

There is a fine difference between the two. A dissent is a privilege extended to members of a council by which they disassociate their names from an action just taken. A protest goes beyond a simple declaration of disagreement to point out that, in the member's estimation, the body has committed a serious constitutional or parliamentary error.

Neither dissents nor protests initiate disciplinary action. They remain in the council's minutes so that, when those minutes are reviewed, the higher council reviewing the minutes may take action to correct the irregularity or delinquency. Both are important avenues for individual expressions of conscience.

Crisis of Conscience: Withdrawal or Renunciation

Should there come a time when the conscience of ordained leaders becomes incompatible with their continuing responsibilities, they are expected to ask that their ordained status be set aside. In the case of ruling elders or deacons, it is the session that accomplishes this action (G-2.0406). In the case of teaching elders, it is the presbytery (G-2.0507).

In either case, the *Book of Order* assumes that a person whose ordered ministry has been set aside will continue to exercise the ordinary ministry of a baptized church member. In the case of teaching elders withdrawing from ordered ministry, the presbytery transfers the individual from its own roll to the roll of one of its congregations.

A far more serious—and irrevocable—step is for a church leader to "renounce the jurisdiction of the church" (G-2.0407, G-2.0509). Whenever a person in ordered ministry communicates such a renunciation of jurisdiction in writing to the clerk of session or the stated clerk of the presbytery, "the renunciation shall be effective upon receipt." There is no further due process, no trial, and no appeal. No concurring vote of the session or presbytery takes place. The clerk simply informs the council that the renunciation has been received, and the person is automatically removed from the roll. The only way for such a person to return to ordered ministry at a later time is through reordination.

Renunciation of jurisdiction is a very serious step with far-reaching ramifications. It should be exercised only by those who are quite sure, beyond all doubt, that their conscience is leading them not only to set aside permanently their ordered ministry, but to cease being Presbyterian as well. Ordained leaders who find themselves in such a quandary are well advised to seek the counsel of their session or presbytery, engaging with them in a season of discernment before taking such an irrevocable step.

Chapter 6

CORPORATE JUDGMENT

> That, in perfect consistency with the above principle of common right, every Christian Church, or union or association of particular churches, is entitled to declare the terms of admission into its communion, and the qualifications of its ministers and members, as well as the whole system of its internal government which Christ hath appointed; that in the exercise of this right they may, notwithstanding, err, in making the terms of communion either too lax or too narrow; yet, even in this case, they do not infringe upon the liberty or the rights of others, but only make an improper use of their own. (F-3.0102)

There is an anecdote, perhaps apocryphal, from the life of Martin Luther that speaks to the issue of boundaries defining church membership. When Luther was a young priest serving his first parish, a dreadful incident took place: the suicide of a teenager. In ministering to the boy's devastated parents, Luther learned that the parish gravedigger had refused to prepare for the young man's interment in the parish cemetery.

This was consistent with official church teachings that declared suicide a mortal sin. Those who died with mortal sins on their souls, the church taught, inevitably went to hell. Although the detrimental effects of other mortal sins could be erased through the sacrament of penance, it was of course a practical impossibility for suicides to confess their sin and perform an act of contrition. The effect of this crushing circular argument was to make suicide an unforgivable sin. The gravedigger was quite right, according to the letter of canon law. The ground inside a churchyard fence was reserved for the saints. Unforgiven mortal sinners had to be buried somewhere else.

Luther, who had a pastor's heart, deeply felt the family's anguish. The 2003 film *Luther*, starring Joseph Fiennes, portrays the cognitive dissonance arising in the young priest's mind over this and similar issues of canon law. Luther has just returned from a pilgrimage to Rome, during which he has witnessed the sale of costly indulgences, even those absolving mortal sins, in exchange for penances no more severe than a whispered prayer before the relic of a saint. Now he has before him the corpse of a deeply troubled soul who was seduced by the twisted, insane logic of suicide—not to mention the young man's heartbroken parents, who have been told they will never see their son again, in this world or the next.

Seething with rage, Luther grabs the gravedigger's shovel. There in the churchyard, he digs the young man's grave himself. Each time the shovel's blade bites into the dry ground, it is as though the reformer is cutting through another level of accumulated legalism. Each shovelful of earth he throws over his shoulder is another stifling, outmoded church law. After gently lowering the boy's body into the grave, Luther defies church tradition by performing a brief service of Christian burial.

This episode may or may not reflect a real historical incident, but it vividly depicts what Luther's career as a Reformer was all about. He challenged the rigid boundaries the medieval church had drawn around salvation, overthrowing its intricate, ingrown, and frequently self-serving system of sins and penance in favor of justification by grace through faith.

Election: Lightly, Like a Thistle

Somewhere in his writings the twentieth-century Reformed theologian Emil Brunner recommends that certain theological terms are best held "lightly, like a thistle." Nowhere is this more true than with the doctrine of election, the question of whom God ultimately chooses to save.

The sixteenth-century Reformed confessions are notable in their reluctance to declare with certainty who does or does not belong to God's elect; and the authors of the Historic Principles follow suit. Election is purely at God's pleasure. It has no relation to any intrinsic human merit. It may never be claimed by anyone on the basis of good behavior. In the words of the Westminster Confession:

> Those of mankind that are predestinated unto life, God, before the foundation of the world was laid, according to his eternal and immutable purpose, and the secret counsel and good pleasure of his will, hath chosen in Christ, unto everlasting glory, out of his free grace and love alone, without any foresight of faith or good works, or perseverance in either of them, or any other thing in the creature, as conditions, or causes moving him thereunto; and all to the praise of his glorious grace. (6.018)

Note the string of qualifying phrases that hammer home, again and again, how election is purely a divine initiative. The Reformers are well aware of how easily predestination can be mishandled, so they hold it gingerly, as if it were a live artillery shell. Predestination, says the Westminster Confession, is a "high mystery [that] is to be handled with special prudence and care" (6.021). Its purpose is not condemnation but assurance: to comfort anxious saints with news of the reasonable likelihood of their salvation. It is not meant to help judgmental believers discern which of their neighbors may not make the cut.

Assurance of salvation, says the Westminster Shorter Catechism, is always hard won, even for the righteous. The personal sense of comfort is fragile. It may come and go:

Assurance of grace and salvation not being of the essence of faith, true believers may wait long before they obtain it; and, after the enjoyment thereof, may have it weakened and intermitted, through manifold distempers, sins, temptations, and desertions; yet are they never left without such a presence and support of the Spirit of God, as keeps them from sinking into utter despair. (7.191)

"Blessed assurance, Jesus is mine," goes Fanny Crosby's nineteenth-century gospel hymn, which is deeply soaked in predestinarian themes. Its words reflect her sheer joy in feeling assured of her election, of receiving a "foretaste of glory divine." This assurance has nothing to do with her own personal virtue, for she is an "heir of salvation," a "purchase of God." The grateful hymn writer knows she has inherited this grace. She has not earned it. She can only practice "perfect submission" to the divine will, knowing "all is at rest."

When it comes to the question of how tightly churches ought to define the boundaries around their own communions, clearly this determination cannot be based on God's election, because no one on this earth can know the details of "God's eternal decrees" (6.014). Even so, in this second Historic Principle, eighteenth-century Presbyterians do assert the church's absolute right to make some provisional judgments. That right, they insist, does not stand in contrast to the first Historic Principle, freedom of conscience. Quite the contrary, it flows from it and stands "in perfect consistency with" it.

With remarkable humility, this second Historic Principle admits the possibility that the church may at times be mistaken in making such judgments. The church "may, notwithstanding, err, in making the terms of communion either too lax or too narrow." Yet, even in the case of such error, those improperly excluded have no recourse. They have no "right to sue," as it were. Their rights have not been violated. They can only speculate that overzealous judges may have made "improper use of their own" rights (F-3.0102).

Yet, as overwhelmingly difficult as it may be to set the boundaries of church membership, it is still a necessary task, in the eyes of the Reformers. Heinrich Bullinger, author of the Second Helvetic Confession, frankly admits the complexity of the task, reminding presbyters of the possibility of error in both directions:

We must not judge rashly or prematurely. Hence we must be very careful not to judge before the time, nor undertake to exclude, reject or cut off those whom the Lord does not want to have excluded or rejected, and those whom we cannot eliminate without loss to the Church. On the other hand, we must be vigilant lest while the pious snore the wicked gain ground and do harm to the Church. (5.140)

The Church, Visible and Invisible

The likelihood that the righteous and the reprobate continue to exist together in the church, side by side, is a reality the Reformers readily admit. Even Jesus says something similar, in relating the parable of the Weeds and the Wheat. Let the weeds grow, knowing that God will eventually separate the two at harvesttime (Matt. 13:24–30).

Following Augustine, the Reformers rely heavily on the distinction between the visible and the invisible church. In his *Institutes*, Calvin observes that the Bible speaks of the church in two ways. The first is "the church which is actually in God's presence, into which no persons are received but those who are children of God by grace of adoption and true members of Christ by sanctification of the Holy Spirit. Then, indeed, the church includes not only the saints presently living on earth, but all the elect from the beginning of the world."

The second is the church as we know it, a very human institution that, while aspiring to holiness, displays telltale signs of impurity deriving from sin: "In this Church are mingled many hypocrites, who have nothing of Christ but the name and outward appearance. There are very many ambitious, greedy, envious persons, evil speakers, and some of quite unclean life. Such are tolerated for a time either because they cannot be convicted by a competent tribunal or because a vigorous discipline does not always flourish as it ought."[1]

Yet even so, says Calvin, we must strive to believe in the spiritual reality of the church, which "is visible to the eyes of God alone, so we are commanded to revere and keep communion with [it]."

For all his high ecclesiology, Calvin is a realist in his pastoral theology. He believes we are able, in this life, only to reach out to the church we do see, the visible church. This flawed and even sinful body of believers admittedly falls short of the heavenly ideal, but it is all we have for the present. By God's grace, it will prove to be enough.

The Westminster Confession echoes Calvin's distinction, describing

---

1. John Calvin, *Institutes of the Christian Religion*, trans. Ford Lewis Battles, ed. John T. McNeill (Louisville, KY: Westminster John Knox Press, 2011), 1021–22, 4.1.7.

the invisible church as a reality that sometimes briefly and tantalizingly displays itself, before obscuring itself once again:

4. This catholic Church hath been sometimes more, sometimes less, visible. And particular churches, which are members thereof, are more or less pure, according as the doctrine of the gospel is taught and embraced, ordinances administered, and public worship performed more or less purely in them.

5. The purest churches under heaven are subject both to mixture and error: and some have so degenerated as to become apparently no churches of Christ. Nevertheless, there shall be always a Church on earth, to worship God according to his will. (6.143-6.144)

This latter idea has come to be known in Reformed circles as "the perseverance of the church" or "the perseverance of the saints." It was a doctrine of great comfort in an era of religious wars, when the obliteration of an entire church body by force of arms seemed a real possibility. It assured beleaguered and persecuted believers that a faithful remnant will always remain, ready to grow again once the Lord wills it.

In modern times, Karl Barth has given the tension between the visible and the invisible church poetic expression, describing theology as "a bird in flight" — in contrast to life in the church, which he ironically describes as more like a bird banging up against the bars of a cage. (Karl Barth, *Evangelical Theology*, trans. Grover Foley [London, 1963], 15)

An Open Table

We have seen how the second Historic Principle speaks frankly of the possibility of error, of "making the terms of communion either too lax or too narrow." There was a time in American Presbyterian history when the pendulum of boundary drawing swung very far in the opposite direction from the open table we know today. That was the era of the communion token.

Common in the nineteenth and early twentieth centuries, communion tokens were a small coin, often of iron or pewter, with the name of a congregation inscribed upon it. Some included a biblical citation such as 1 Corinthians 11:28: "Examine yourselves, and only then eat of the bread and drink of the cup." Here the apostle is admonishing believers to take special care not to come to the table unworthily, lest they "eat and drink judgment against themselves."

Reacting against the sacramental laxity of medieval Roman Catholicism, in which the faithful sometimes partook of the communion wafer with a minimal, even magical, understanding of the sacrament, the Reformers who followed Calvin called for the Lord's Supper to be celebrated less frequently, so as to allow for a more careful approach. This was despite Calvin's insistence that the Lord's Supper be celebrated weekly. Sometimes the sacrament was celebrated as infrequently as twice a year. Before each administration of the sacrament, worshipers were required to first attend a penitential service at which they publicly and collectively confessed their sins. The intent was to institutionalize the sort of earnest self-examination Paul is recommending. The penitential service—often held on a Friday evening—lasted as long as several hours.

At the conclusion of the penitential service, those present were given a communion token, which they were directed to bring to the sanctuary as they returned for worship on the Lord's Day. At the Sunday service, only those with tokens in hand—indicating that they had properly prepared themselves spiritually—were permitted to receive the communion elements.

Today communion tokens belong to the realm of coin collectors, but in their heyday they were a notable symbol of Presbyterian life. The twenty-first-century church, of course, operates under a distinctly different sacramental theology that is more in line with Calvin's original vision. As the Directory for Worship insists, "All the baptized faithful are to be welcomed to the Table, and none shall be excluded because of race, sex, age, economic status, social class, handicapping condition, difference of culture or language, or any barrier created by human injustice" (W-2.4006).

Not a word is said about barring the table for any reason other than baptism. Because baptism is the basic mark of membership in Christ's church, the Lord's Table is open to all Christian believers. A proposed revision to the Directory for Worship, to be presented to the General Assembly in 2016, moves even further in the direction of a completely open table. This change would allow unbaptized seekers to be admitted to the table, as long as an invitation to be baptized at a later date is extended to them.

Was the practice of fencing the table an example of making the terms of communion "too narrow"? Most contemporary Presbyterians would unreservedly answer yes. Many American Presbyterians of the mid-nineteenth century, by contrast, would be appalled by today's open table, thinking it an example of rules that are "too lax." This is an example of how the Historic Principles provide general theological guidance that informs more specific rubrics that follow. Presbyterian polity is a living tradition, constantly being reinterpreted and refashioned to meet the needs of new generations.

Becoming a Church Member

The second Historic Principle speaks also of the church's right to determine "the qualifications of its ministers and members." With respect to church membership, the arena where that decision making happens is the session.

The general principle guiding sessions in making such decisions is one of welcome and openness: "A congregation shall welcome all persons who trust in God's grace in Jesus Christ and desire to become part of the fellowship and ministry of his Church" (F-1.0403). "No person shall be denied membership for any reason not related to profession of faith. The Gospel leads members to extend the fellowship of Christ to all persons. Failure to do so constitutes a rejection of Christ himself and causes a scandal to the Gospel" (G-1.0302).

While that may sound perfectly commonplace today, there have been times in Presbyterian Church history in which such a principle could not have been taken for granted, particularly with respect to racial divisions. Today, the explicit language of full welcome to all who confess faith in Jesus Christ is the unquestionable standard.

The Form of Government sets the church-membership bar intentionally low, for the sake of evangelism. Profession of faith is the sole criterion. Although higher standards pertain for those ordained as deacons and ruling elders, church members are expected only to demonstrate their sincere desire to follow Christ, and that they are willing to receive the sacrament of baptism if they have not done so already. This is not, of course, to say there is nothing more to being a faithful Christian than answering a few questions during a worship service. It is merely a practical recognition that public profession of faith is the starting point.

There are three ways to join a Presbyterian church:

a. *Public profession of faith,* made after careful examination by the session in the meaning and responsibilities of membership; if not already baptized, the person making profession of faith shall be baptized;

With respect to the membership of presbyteries—whose permanent members are primarily teaching elders—a whole different set of standards applies. An entire section of the Form of Government is devoted to outlining a standard Preparation for Ministry Process, requiring a three-year Master of Divinity degree, including courses in biblical languages (G-2.06). Even with these rigorous requirements, the ultimate right of approval—both for the newly ordained and for those entering a presbytery by transfer—rests with the presbytery: "Teaching elders have membership in the presbytery by action of the presbytery itself, and no pastoral relationship may be established, changed, or dissolved without the approval of the presbytery" (G-2.0502)

b. *Certificate of transfer,* when a person is a member of another Christian church at the time of transfer;

c. *Reaffirmation of faith,* for persons previously baptized in the name of the triune God and having publicly professed their faith. (G-1.0303)

Receiving a new member by public profession of faith is a special joy. Generally these are either adults who are becoming Christian disciples for the first time or youth who have been nurtured in the church and are ready to confirm the promises their parents or guardians made on their behalf at baptism (W-4.2003). In either case, it is wise for sessions to arrange for a program of instruction followed by examination, so they can satisfy themselves that the new members are serious in their commitment and prepared to make a public profession of faith. Sessions may either conduct this examination directly or by means of a commission elected for that purpose. This program of instruction, historically known as catechesis, is one of the oldest traditions of the Christian church.

Although the Roman Catholic and Anglican traditions consider confirmation to be a sacrament, in the Presbyterian Church it is functionally no different than becoming an active church member. Presbyterians speak of "confirmation and commissioning" together (W-4.2003); this includes both a look backward to the original baptismal promises and a look forward to the new work of discipleship for which these new members are commissioned.

While sessions may add additional creedal requirements to this basic profession of faith, few do. Following the example of Jesus himself, who called disciples to himself with the simple invitation, "Follow me," wise session members understand that the Christian journey proceeds one step at a time. This first and most essential step toward discipleship, as Calvin points out, is a commitment of the heart: "It is a doctrine not of the tongue, but of life. It is not apprehended by the understanding and memory alone, as other disciplines are, but it is received only when it possesses the whole soul, and finds a seat and resting place in the inmost affection of the heart" (John Calvin, *Institutes,* vol. 1; 3.6.4).

A common misconception about certificates of transfer—often called "letters of transfer"—is that sessions store letters of recommendation for each of their members in a file, that they release to another congregation when the member transfers. Sometimes members will ask that "their letter" be handed over to them, so they may present it to the new congregation. This is not the way membership transfers work. Certificates of transfer are issued by the former church only at the request of the clerk of session (or similar official) of the new congregation, after the transferring members have expressed a desire to join. A request for a certificate of transfer is essentially a courtesy the new church extends to the former one, notifying them it is time to remove the transferring member's name from their roll.

Reaffirmation of faith is appropriate for all others who have previously made a public profession of faith but for whom a certificate of transfer cannot be obtained. This may be because the former church does not issue letters of transfer or because the new members allowed their membership in their former church to lapse.

Whichever of these three ways a new member is received, the distinction is only significant on the occasion of their joining. Other than a notation in the session minutes, there is typically no record kept, after the fact, of the way in which a person became a member. While some may regard one means of joining as more prestigious than another, there are in fact no grades nor degrees within the category of membership. All are equal before Christ: sinners who depend on nothing but unmerited grace to be justified.

Baptism and Membership

At one time, when the surrounding culture was heavily churched, adult professions of faith with baptism were relatively rare. As the culture has become more secular, and the numbers of unaffiliated people who consider themselves "spiritual but not religious" increases, adult baptisms are becoming more common.

Sometimes it happens that new members are uncertain whether or not they have been baptized. In such a case, inquiries should be made with the parents or guardians, adoption-agency or foster-care administrators, or churches they formerly attended, to determine if records of a baptism exist. If the search comes up empty, the best course of action is to proceed with the baptism anyway, using a provisional baptismal formula that begins "If you have not previously been baptized," taking care to explain to the congregation the reason for the unusual language. While it is irregular for a person to be baptized more than once, it would be an even greater irregularity to omit baptism entirely.

While nearly every Christian church practices baptism in some form, there

It is wrong to speak of adult baptisms, implying that they are different from infant baptisms. Although the baptism of adults is accompanied by their profession of faith, the sacrament itself is no different. It is especially inappropriate to refer to the Sacrament of Infant Baptism or the Sacrament of Adult Baptism in church newsletters or worship orders. The Sacrament of Baptism is sufficient, whatever the age of the person being baptized.

are a few cases of Christian churches—such as the Society of Friends or Quakers—who do not. Prior membership in one of those churches could result in a situation in which a person has made a public profession of faith but remains unbaptized. In such cases, the transferring member should be baptized anyway.

Baptism is the most ecumenical of sacraments. As a result of the Donatist controversy in the fourth century, the Christian church established the principle that all baptisms with water, celebrated in the name of the triune God, are valid. Consequently, baptisms meeting those two criteria are broadly recognized as valid by the vast majority of Christian denominations, including the Roman Catholic Church. Although churches in the Anabaptist tradition often refuse to recognize infant baptisms (because they were not accompanied by a profession of faith by the person being baptized), the opposite is not the case. Presbyterians gladly recognize baptisms performed by Anabaptist churches, or any other church whose baptismal ceremony meets the two criteria. It should be noted that Presbyterians do not recognize baptisms performed by the Church of Jesus Christ of Latter-day Saints (the Mormons) because that church's understanding of the interrelationship of the three persons of the Trinity is so different.

"The Meaning of Membership and Baptism" (G-1.0301) contains a number of important principles:

> In Jesus Christ, God calls people to faith and to membership in the Church, the body of Christ. Baptism is the visible sign of that call and claim on a human life and of entrance into the membership of the church. The baptism of children witnesses to the truth that God's love claims people before they are able to respond in faith. The baptism of those who enter the covenant of membership upon their own profession of faith in Jesus Christ as Lord and Savior witnesses to the truth that God's gift of grace calls forth a response of faithfulness.

The first line speaks of how, in Christ, "God calls people to faith and to membership in the church." It is worth noting, in this increasingly unchurched culture, that the *Book of Order* inextricably links faith and church membership. This is a natural expression of the Reformed tradition's high conception of the church. To Reformed Christians, the church—the body of Christ—is not incidental to faith. So closely is the church tied to the life of faith that it is impossible to conceive of Christianity being practiced apart from a worshiping congregation.

To be sure, there are extreme examples of circumstances that, on rare occasions, force believers to live in isolation from others. Of course God continues to be present to prisoners in solitary confinement and to scientists wintering in Antarctica. There is also a rich tradition of hermitage within Christian spirituality, by which certain individuals vow to live for a time in contemplative seclusion. Yet even these godly hermits typically view their solitude as enfolded within the larger fellowship of the church. A monk belonging to a contemplative religious order who spends decades in a hermit's cell remains a member of the community.

The situation of a Christian who, as a matter of personal preference, simply declines to affiliate with other believers in community is very different. This is an increasingly common lifestyle choice in this individualistic culture, which idolizes self-sufficiency. As the Reformed tradition sees it, Christians who forsake involvement in any sort of church are unwittingly forsaking Christianity as well. Decades of televised football-stadium evangelistic services have, for many, reduced the essential Protestant teaching of justification by grace through faith into a formulaic "decision for Christ" while neglecting to emphasize that this is, necessarily, a decision to follow Christ, in community. The Presbyterian response to such self-imposed isolation can only be a warm, heartfelt, and repeated invitation to membership.

The apostle Paul expresses a high conception of church membership as he declares that "the eye cannot say to the hand, 'I have no need of you'" (1 Cor. 12:21). No doubt there are at least as many people in twenty-first-century America professing to live the life of that self-sufficient, disembodied eye as there were in first-century Corinth.

Baptism implies church membership. Even newly baptized infants, who are in no way able to respond to the call to Christian community, are listed on the church's roll of baptized members. For years before they make their own profession of faith and confirm the promises made at their baptism, those listed on this roll are members of the church.

Only in the most unusual circumstances do Presbyterian ministers perform baptisms outside the context of common worship, in settings such as hospital rooms. Other than such rare pastoral-care situations, baptisms must be authorized by the session and celebrated in the context of Christian worship (W-2.3011). In these unusual situations, the *Book of Order* enjoins teaching elders to immediately "take responsibility that the newly baptized person is enrolled as a member of a particular church" (W-2.3011b).

It is wise to avoid describing confirmation as the time when young people "join the church." If confirmands have been baptized, they are already members.

By the same token, *church membership implies baptism.* No one becomes a member of the church without first having been baptized, either on some earlier occasion or at the time of public profession of faith.

Responsibilities of Church Members

"The Ministry of Members," G-1.0304, can be described as the job description of a church member. Assuming a role of active engagement in the church's mission, this section outlines the following specific responsibilities:

- proclaiming the good news in word and deed,
- taking part in the common life and worship of a congregation,
- lifting one another up in prayer, mutual concern, and active support,
- studying Scripture and the issues of Christian faith and life,
- supporting the ministry of the church through the giving of money, time, and talents,
- demonstrating a new quality of life within and through the church,
- responding to God's activity in the world through service to others,
- living responsibly in the personal, family, vocational, political, cultural, and social relationships of life,
- working in the world for peace, justice, freedom, and human fulfillment,
- participating in the governing responsibilities of the church, and
- reviewing and evaluating regularly the integrity of one's membership, and considering ways in which one's participation in the worship and service of the church may be increased and made more meaningful.

It can be a useful exercise to hand out copies of this list at new-member training. Some elements of the list may come as a surprise: for example, "proclaiming the good news in word and deed." Although few church members will ever be called upon to deliver a sermon, life affords ample, less formal opportunities for sharing the good news—with the most effective witness often taking the form of deeds rather than words.

"Studying scripture and the issues of Christian faith and life" may come as a surprise to others, who have mistakenly assumed their Christian education ended in their childhood. Presbyterians have a long tradition of emphasizing education for all ages.

"Taking part in the common life and worship of a congregation" is left up to local sessions to define more precisely. How frequently is a church member expected to join in corporate worship? Every Lord's Day is surely the ideal, but—judging from the gap in most congregations between average worship attendance and the membership roll—there is always room for growth. As for common life, that phrase is undefined but bears witness to the fact that there is a good deal more to congregational life than attending worship services.

For savvy consumers who are schooled to seek out the financial "bottom line" in any and all circumstances, "supporting the ministry of the church through the giving of money, time, and talents" stands out like a red flag. Some new members, particularly those from unchurched backgrounds, may ask "how much it costs" to belong to the church or what the membership dues are. The short answer is that following Jesus Christ costs everything we have and are, requiring us to share talents and abilities as well as financial resources. Individual sessions will have their own take on how important it is to emphasize the biblical tithe (10 percent of gross income) in the membership-training context, but surely all teach proportionate (percentage) giving to some degree.

The phrase "a new quality of life" may sound at first like an airy platitude, but it may help to ask the new-members class to list some ways Christians are meant to live differently from their neighbors. (Does it make a difference to the neighbors if we are members of a church? Do they even know we are Christians? If not, why not?)

Several items on the list allude to the specific work of discipleship: "service to others," "living responsibly" in varied personal and professional relationships, and "working in the world for peace, justice, freedom, and human fulfillment." While some of these items may verge on the platitudinous, collectively they bear witness to the call of all church members to be missionaries in their own setting.

"Participating in the governing responsibilities of the church" presents a blank slate to those not already schooled in Presbyterianism, but this item provides an opportunity to do some teaching about church government, particularly the importance of participating in congregational meetings. It also may surprise some new members to consider that they too could one day be nominated and elected to be ordained as deacons or ruling elders, or perhaps be called by God to become a teaching elder.

The final item, "reviewing and evaluating regularly the integrity of one's membership," places the responsibility for self-assessment squarely on the shoulders of church members. It may be useful for sessions to plan some sort of annual occasion to encourage such introspection, perhaps a service of renewal of baptismal promises such as the one found in the *Book of Common Worship*.

Categories of Membership

At the time of its adoption, one of the most-discussed features of the present Form of Government was the removal of the category of inactive member. This reduced the number of required membership rolls from four to three (Active Members, Baptized Members, and Affiliate Members).

Baptized Members are those who have received the sacrament of baptism but have not yet made a public profession of faith (G-1.0401). Affiliate Member is a flexible category sessions may use to include people who are active members of another congregation but are living in their community temporarily. Examples include college students, those serving in the military, and "snowbirds" who relocate seasonally to a second home.

Many sessions continue to use an Inactive Roll as a tool for ministry. The *Book of Order* is permissive on that point, allowing flexibility at the local level. Sessions who decide to maintain an Inactive Roll should be aware that, in moving names off the Active Roll, they must cease including such individuals in the annual membership count they submit to the General Assembly, through their presbytery. For all practical purposes, inactive members are no longer members of the Presbyterian Church (U.S.A.), even though leaders of the congregation may continue to refer to them as members, at their option. The church should certainly continue to extend pastoral care. Should a future request arise to issue a letter of transfer for someone on an Inactive Roll, sessions can only accomplish this by first restoring them to the Active Roll.

Ecumenical Relationships

Parallel to the Presbyterian Church's right to declare "the terms of admission into its communion" is its interest in maintaining ecumenical relationships. In G-5.0101, "Ecumenicity," the church pledges "at all levels [to seek] to manifest more visibly the unity of the body of Christ," meaning it "will seek to initiate, maintain, and strengthen relations with other Reformed and Christian entities." Note that the unity of the body of Christ is not something the church itself creates. Unity is already present, wherever Christ is. Our mission is to move beyond the easy familiarity of settings where everyone acts and thinks and worships as we do to follow the one whose heartfelt prayer is "that they may all be one" (John 17:21).

The same is true for interfaith conversations (G-5.0102) and even dialogue with "secular organizations and agencies where such approaches show promise of serving the mission of the Church in the world" (G-5.0103). The wise words of the Pharisee Gamaliel in Acts 5 provide a model for cooperation with agencies that are doing godly work but that stop short of doing so in the name of Christ: "If this plan or this undertaking is of human origin, it will fail; but if it is of God, you will not be able to overthrow them—in that case you may even be found fighting against God!" (Acts 5:38b–39).

But the *Book of Order* calls Presbyterians to more than just the benign neglect Gamaliel advises. The challenge is to venture outside the doors of the sanctuary—to the other side of the stained glass—to share community and conversation with those who have a heart for the same good works the Scriptures teach.

This movement toward institutional unity is consistent with the Confession of 1967, which affirms, "The institutions of the people of God change and vary as their mission requires in different times and places. The unity of the church is compatible with a wide variety of forms, but it is hidden and distorted when variant forms are allowed to harden into sectarian divisions, exclusive denominations, and rival factions" (9.34).

With respect to ecumenical relationships, the basic standard is that the Presbyterian Church (U.S.A.) seeks to be at least in "a relationship of correspondence" with other denominations (G-5.0201). The stated clerk of the General Assembly maintains a list of those churches who currently share that negotiated mutual agreement with Presbyterians.

Denominations in ecumenical correspondence may agree to recognize the validity of one another's baptisms and also to allow for the orderly transfer of those ordained as teaching elders or their equivalents, whenever the mission of both churches warrants it. With the full agreement of the regional councils of both denominations, Presbyterian teaching elders may receive calls from congregations of denominations in ecumenical correspondence. This requires leaving the Presbyterian Church (U.S.A.) for the other denomination. The advantage of the ecumenical correspondence relationship—as opposed to denominations with which the Presbyterian Church (U.S.A.) does not share any such relationship—is that the transferring minister's ordination may be recognized and brought into the new denomination (some further study and examination may still be required, in order to demonstrate familiarity with the new denomination's theology, polity, and traditions). The alternative would be to surrender one's ordination, then complete the other denomination's preparation-for-ministry process and be reordained.

A higher standard is evident in the relationship known as full communion, based on mutual agreements negotiated by the Presbyterian Church (U.S.A.) and other Christian bodies (G-5.0202). Examples are the four-way *Formula of Agreement*, finalized in 1998, among the Presbyterians, the Evangelical Lutheran Church in America, the Reformed Church in America, and the United Church of Christ, and the similar 2011 agreement with the Moravian Church in North America. Beyond merely recognizing one another's essential unity in Christ, the *Formula of Agreement* allows for ministers from one of these denominations to accept calls from Presbyterian congregations without having to leave their own denomination, and vice versa. Such teaching elders are enrolled as temporary members of the presbytery for the duration of their service (G-2.0506).

Chapter 5 of the Form of Government concludes by sketching out two possible road maps for the future in pursuit of deeper Christian unity. The first is easy to describe but much more difficult to attain: "full organic union" (G-5.03). It is precisely what it describes: total merger of the Presbyterian Church (U.S.A.) with another denomination.

The second road map carries forward a wise approach from the past that may yet prove useful in future union negotiations. Union presbyteries (G-5.04) were a key feature of Presbyterian life in the years leading up to the 1983 reunion of the Presbyterian Church in the U.S. and the United Presbyterian Church in the U.S.A. Having failed on earlier occasions to attain organic union, those working toward unity pursued a gradual approach of creating "union presbyteries." Essentially, this was a cautious, slow-motion denominational union that took place over several decades. Presbyteries located in states that had significant numbers of congregations of both denominations agreed to enter into union with each other. These union presbyteries were related to both denominations. By the time the two denominations again took up the question of union in the early 1980s, it was no longer an issue for Presbyterians in the union presbyteries, because their members were already practicing reunion on the presbytery level. The authorization for union presbyteries continues to be part of the *Constitution*: an ecumenical tool ready to be dusted off and used again, should it prove useful.

Chapter 7

MINISTRY

That our blessed Savior, for the edification of the visible Church, which is his body, hath appointed officers, not only to preach the gospel and administer the Sacraments, but also to exercise discipline, for the preservation of both truth and duty; and that it is incumbent upon these officers, and upon the whole Church, in whose name they act, to censure or cast out the erroneous and scandalous, observing, in all cases, the rules contained in the Word of God. (F-3.0103)

Based on our best understanding of the Bible and early church history, there are certain problems with the third Historic Principle, the one dealing with officers. John Calvin, along with his eighteenth-century theological heirs who drafted the Historic Principles, understood the formation of the early Christian church in ways we now know to be unhistorical. Eager to debunk the traditional Roman Catholic claim that Jesus established the medieval papacy when he said, "You are Peter, and on this rock I will build my church" (Matt. 16:18), Calvin presented an alternative narrative based on the best biblical scholarship of his day. This model had Paul replicating a uniform pattern of governance by presbyters and deacons that, Calvin believed, had originally been established by Jesus himself. John Knox took this Calvinist pattern of ministry to Scotland, whence it made its way to the New World.

In the Gospels, Jesus almost never talks about the church. The only places in which Jesus is recorded as uttering the word *ekklesia* are both in the Gospel of Matthew. In Matthew 16:18 he calls Peter the rock on which he will build his church, and in Matthew 18:17 he instructs a person with a grievance first to seek out the brother who caused the offense, and if that is not successful, then to "tell it to the church." There is strong reason to suspect, on linguistic and historical grounds, that both these statements are later interpolations. They are simply not consistent with Jesus' mission, as we read about it elsewhere in the New Testament. The Jesus of Scripture is far more concerned with drawing attention to the inbreaking reign of God than he is with establishing any human institution.

The only institution Jesus is recorded as establishing is the little band of disciples he gathers around him: twelve in number, according to some accounts (corresponding to the twelve tribes of Israel), but also differing in number in other accounts. In Luke 10:1–12, Jesus commissions "the seventy." There appear to have been other leaders as well, including Mary Magdalene and other women—although the later church likely suppressed the record of their leading roles. When a couple of Jesus' followers, James and John, make a bid for the corner office, he rebuffs them in the strongest possible terms, holding up sanctified slavery (*diakonia*) as the ideal (Mark 10:35–45). This diverse and varied Gospel record is hardly the firm polity foundation Calvin believed he discerned in the Scriptures and in the writings of early church leaders.

The only possible conclusion is that Luther, Calvin, and the other Protestant Reformers, as intellectually brilliant as they were, were working with biblical source materials that are dated a good deal later than they ever imagined and that depict a more parochial understanding of the polity of the early church than they ever realized. The clear pattern they thought they discerned in the pages of the Pastoral Epistles was by no means passed on directly from Jesus to the apostles as a universal pattern.

If Presbyterians can no longer see their polity clearly emerging from the pages of the New Testament, then it does not appear that any other denomination can, either. Those early decades, devoted as they were to the urgent priorities of evangelization and surviving Roman persecution, were not a time when questions of church order loomed large in anyone's minds.

As for Paul, once we understand the Pastoral Epistles to be significantly later documents that were not authored by him, the record that remains in his genuine letters demonstrates a loose, charismatic church order. There is no question Paul established churches, but he seems to have understood church order as having been provided on the fly by the Holy Spirit, in support of his itinerant mission. The Paul we read about in the epistles clearly authored by him and in the Acts of the Apostles is a man on the move who has little time for the fine details of church government.

The best understanding we have of first-century church order, therefore, is sketchy at best. Once it became apparent Christ's return was not likely to be imminent, church order seems to have developed virally, in ad hoc fashion, in numerous locations at the same time. In those early years it was not always clear, in every place, that a given community was in fact a Christian church, rather than a reformed Jewish sect. In some locations, ecclesiastical self-awareness seems to have grown more rapidly than in others.

There is evidence in the Acts of the Apostles and in the New Testament letters authored by Paul that Jesus' brother James, assisted by Peter, exercised some oversight in the earliest years, but such central organization evidently did not survive the Roman attack that destroyed Jerusalem in 70 CE. The structure that emerges in the Pastoral Epistles—Calvin's principal source—is a late-first-century accommodation to the need for order in Christian Diaspora communities that had suddenly and unexpectedly lost touch with the home office. The Pastorals shed much light on church life in a few cities toward the end of the first century, but they cannot provide the sort of universal blueprint for Presbyterian polity, established by Jesus, that the Genevan reformer imagined he discovered in their pages.

When the third Historic Principle claims that "our blessed Savior, for the edification of the visible Church, which is his body, hath appointed officers," we cannot understand that statement to refer to teachings of the historical Jesus, transmitted to his disciples. Rather, it is a faith statement, confessing that Christ, the risen and reigning Lord, through the Holy Spirit, guided the Christian community as church order developed throughout those chaotic early centuries.

Diakonia

The section of the Form of Government dealing with ministerial order takes an approach more consistent with recent historical-critical study of the Bible than does the third Historic Principle. Rather than portraying Jesus as the architect of Presbyterian polity, it focuses on the style of ministry he evidences in the Gospels. As James and John learned from their Lord's abrupt answer to their bid for primacy, this is servant ministry through and through:

> The Church's ministry is a gift from Jesus Christ to the whole Church. Christ alone rules, calls, teaches, and uses the Church as he wills, exercising his authority by the ministry of women and men for the establishment and extension of God's new creation. Christ's ministry is the foundation and standard for all ministry, the pattern of the one who came "not to be served but to serve" (Matt. 20:28). The basic form of ministry is the ministry of the whole people of God, from whose midst some are called to ordered ministries, to fulfill particular functions. Members and those in ordered ministries serve together under the mandate of Christ (G-2.0101).

Ministry after the example of Jesus Christ, whatever particular form or order it takes, displays a certain character akin to DNA. The fundamental organizational pattern running through all faithful Christian ministry—whatever outward, official form it may assume—is *diakonia*, or servanthood. The fact that biblical translators variously render *diakonos* as "minister," "deacon," or "servant" is based on scant linguistic evidence, heavily influenced by later church tradition. It is possible, even likely, that the New Testament authors—with the possible exception of the Pastoral

Epistles—simply meant to say "servant" in every such case, without iden-
tifying an established office bearing that name.

Can we imagine an early church governed, in large part, by "servants,"
without a full-blown system of ordered ministry? It seems likely the New
Testament authors could.

As a theological thought experiment, try rewriting the first part of the
third Historic Principle, substituting the word "servant" every place the
word "officer" appears. It would read like this:

That our blessed Savior, for the edification of the visible Church,
which is his body, hath appointed *servants*, not only to preach the gospel and administer the Sacraments, but also to exercise discipline, for
the preservation of both truth and duty; and that it is incumbent upon
these *servants*, and upon the whole Church, in whose name they act,
to censure or cast out the erroneous and scandalous, observing, in all
cases, the rules contained in the Word of God. (F-3.0103)

Because servanthood is clearly the defining model for leadership in
the teachings of both Jesus and Paul, there is no question that it must
serve as the underlying theological foundation for ordered ministry in the
Reformed tradition. Despite the dated occurrences of the word "office" in
the third Historic Principle, the truly Reformed understanding of ministry
is not official at all, but functional. Tasks arise in the church, and the Holy
Spirit calls forth faithful servants to perform them. This is the essence of
biblically faithful ministry.

Ordered Ministry

Note, however, that Reformed ministry is also *ordered* ministry. The very
book that outlines the polity of the church is called the *Book of Order*. It lays
out the rudiments of ministerial order as follows:

The Church's ordered ministries described in the New Testament
and maintained by this church are deacons and presbyters (teaching
elders and ruling elders). Ordered ministries are gifts to the church
to order its life so that the ministry of the whole people of God may
flourish. The existence of these ordered ministries in no way dimin-
ishes the importance of the commitment of all members to the total
ministry of the church. (G-2.0102)

The understanding of ministerial order laid out here is threefold—deacons, teaching elders, and ruling elders—even though two of these are
described as subsets of a larger class, presbyters. The current ecumenical

consensus, based on the *Baptism, Eucharist and Ministry (BEM)* document of the World Council of Churches, is that classical Christian ministerial order is likewise threefold, following the pattern of bishop, presbyter, and deacon.

While the Presbyterian order of deacon corresponds simply and easily to the *BEM* pattern, there is no similarly precise correspondence of ruling elders and teaching elders. While both of these can be said to belong to the *BEM* order of presbyter, there are in fact elements of both that also correspond to the order of bishop—a term that has historically been fraught with difficulty for Presbyterians, due to painful memories of the lengthy and sometimes bloody struggle against episcopal rule in Europe, particularly Scotland.

The historic hallmarks of the Roman Catholic bishop's office have been (1) responsibility for the proclamation of the Word and the celebration of the sacraments in a given area and (2) regional ecclesiastical governance. Bishops are assisted by presbyters (priests), who extend the ministry of word and sacrament from the episcopal cathedral into their local parishes. The word "cathedral" literally means "chair" and refers to the chair occupied by the bishop at the celebration of the mass—underlining the liturgical nature of the bishop's role.

In the Presbyterian system, there is no cathedral, nor is there a single individual bearing the title of bishop. Teaching elders serving as pastors exercise an episcopal role when they proclaim the Word and celebrate the sacraments in a congregation. That role is different from that of Roman Catholic priests, who exercise such functions as presbyters, under the strict guidance and control of their bishops. Roman Catholic priests, in this way of thinking, function more like what Presbyterians know as Ruling Elders Commissioned to Particular Pastoral Service (G-2.1002).

Presbyterian pastors, by contrast, are given broad personal authority to decide questions such as which Scripture passages are read (whether from a lectionary or not), from which translation those readings come (W-2.2005), what the topic of the sermon will be, what music is sung, what prayers are offered, and what other artistic forms are appropriate (W-1.4005). This is episcopal authority, according to the classic definition, and it extends far beyond the decision-making authority typically accorded to Roman Catholic priests—whose bishops make most such decisions for them, in the form of a centrally printed "missalette," or seasonal collection of worship resources. Indeed, it was common practice in American Presbyterianism, well into the nineteenth century, to use the word "bishop" as an alternative title for minister of the Word.

The following description of the duties of teaching elders outlines certain functions that are necessarily lodged in a person, rather than in a church council:

Teaching elders (also called ministers of the Word and Sacrament) shall in all things be committed to teaching the faith and equipping the saints for the work of ministry (Eph. 4:12). . . . When they serve as preachers and teachers of the Word, they shall preach and teach the faith of the church, so that the people are shaped by the pattern of the gospel and strengthened for witness and service. When they serve at font and table, they shall interpret the mysteries of grace and lift the people's vision toward the hope of God's new creation. When they serve as pastors, they shall support the people in the disciplines of the faith amid the struggles of daily life. When they serve as presbyters, they shall participate in the responsibilities of governance, seeking always to discern the mind of Christ and to build up Christ's body through devotion, debate, and decision. (G-2.0501)

This passage displays the limitations of the term "teaching elder" in describing the fullness of the pastor's role. "Participating in the responsibilities of governance" is but one duty attached to this position. It appears last on the list and—judging from the language used to describe it—it appears to be of least importance. "Preaching and teaching the faith of the church," "interpreting the mysteries of grace and lifting the people's vision," "supporting the people in the disciplines of the faith amid the struggles of daily life" are classic episcopal functions, according to the best and oldest understanding of the word "bishop."

The second aspect of classic episcopal authority, according to the *BEM* model, is that of governance. Presbyteries are sometimes described as a "corporate bishop": the governance decisions made by a single individual in the Roman Catholic system are made, instead, by a corporate legislative body. This is where the final item in G-2.0501's list of ministerial responsibilities comes into play: "participating in the responsibilities of governance, seeking always to discern the mind of Christ and to build up Christ's body through devotion, debate, and decision."

Censuring and Casting Out

Few men and women today, discerning God's call to become either teaching or ruling elders, think much about the responsibilities they take on "to censure or cast out the erroneous and scandalous" (in the language of the third Historic Principle). Presbyterian churches in twenty-first-century America function, for all practical purposes, as voluntary organizations. They have nothing of the legally established character that churches once had in Calvin's Geneva or Knox's Edinburgh.

Those churches functioned as close partners with the secular governing authorities. In earlier times, the censure of an ecclesiastical body brought public humiliation that deterred crime and other misbehavior. Today, with the separation of church and state, a local church's public censure of one of its members would likely elicit little more than a peevish decision to quit that church for a congregation of another denomination.

However, within the community of the church, presbyters do have a role to play in administering the Rules of Discipline. Although its provisions are rarely exercised, when they are truly needed—and when both parties to a dispute remain in the church and see the process through—the Rules are still a powerful tool for discerning God's will and administering justice.

The disciplinary function of ordained leaders is described more fully in chapter 12, on Ecclesiastical Discipline.

The Call

At the heart of the Reformed understanding of ministry, for all three ordered ministries, is a call from God, which must be confirmed by a church council. A call to ordained service has two components, an inner call and an outer call.

The inner call belongs to the realm of spirituality, to the person's inner life. The church is always interested in hearing its ordained leaders share their sense of calling in the form of personal testimony, but naturally it has few ways of assessing the validity of private spiritual experiences. What the church *is* able to do is to identify the fruits of the inner call, qualifying the person for ordained service through what the Reformers historically called "the acclamation of the people."

This acclamation is the outer call. In the case of deacons and ruling elders, the acclamation of the people takes the form of nomination in a

---

The following selection from the Second Helvetic Confession—dating from an era in which only men were considered for ordained service—is one of many that provides general guidance to ordaining councils as they ponder whether or not to affirm the outer call:

> But let the ministers of the Church be called and chosen by lawful and ecclesiastical election; that is to say, let them be carefully chosen by the Church or by those delegated from the Church for that purpose in a proper order without any uproar, dissension and rivalry. Not any one may be elected, but capable men distinguished by sufficient consecrated learning, pious eloquence, simple wisdom, lastly, by moderation and an honorable reputation, according to that apostolic rule which is compiled by the apostle in 1 Tim., ch. 3, and Titus, ch. 1. (5.150)

congregational meeting, followed by a vote to extend a call, followed in turn by the session's examination and approval. In the case of teaching elders, the acclamation of the people takes the form of nomination by a pastor nominating committee, followed by a congregational vote to extend a call, followed in turn by the presbytery's examination and approval. Teaching elders serving in specialized ministries do so at the exclusive bidding of the presbytery, so there is no congregational participation. In such cases, the outer call comes through the presbytery alone, as it assesses missional needs within its region—although the presbytery may take into account testimony from the employing organization, if there is one.

Ideally, the inner call and the outer call are of equal importance. In practice, some may mistakenly ascribe greater importance to one. In the case of deacons and ruling elders, there is often a tendency to overemphasize the outer call. A member of a congregational nominating committee will contact a church member, saying, "We think you would make an ideal deacon." It is not so common for the committee member to say, "We're wondering if you have been sensing God leading you to become a deacon." In the case of teaching elders, a surprising number of men and women enroll in seminary as a response to their personal sense of God's calling, without first seeking the affirmation of their session and presbytery by enrolling as inquirers. If seminarians have only a short history of active involvement as church members, they may be inclined to view the presbytery's preparation-for-ministry process as a series of hoops to jump through rather than the partnership of prayerful mutual discernment it is intended to be.

Qualifications for Ordained Service

The church's qualifications for ordained service—its ordination standards—have been the subject of intense debate for a generation or more. The debate has centered around the suitability for ordination of those in

William Chapman provides helpful historical perspective as he observes that this is not the first time the church has lived through a grueling season of controversy with respect to the manner of life that ought to be displayed by its ordained leaders. The General Assembly has, in the past, offered similar authoritative interpretations with respect to the drinking of "ardent spirits" (1811–1880) and the use of tobacco (1916), denying scholarship money to those who refused to comply. In each instance, later actions of the General Assembly removed those restrictions.

—William Chapman, *History and Theology in the* Book of Order: *Blood on Every Page* (Witherspoon Press, 1999), 37.

same-sex relationships. For more than forty years, beginning in the 1970s, the General Assembly issued various authoritative interpretations of the *Constitution* declaring that "self-avowed, practicing homosexuals" are not suitable for ordination. That declaration made a distinction between homosexual orientation and homosexual practice, tying the ordination prohibition only to actions rather than inner inclinations.

In 1997, knowing that a simple majority vote of a General Assembly was all that was needed to overturn a previous authoritative interpretation, some who feared a change in the ordination standards proposed a constitutional amendment. Amendments require not only a majority vote of the General Assembly, but also a concurring vote of a majority of the presbyteries. The Assembly approved the amendment, and a year later a new paragraph was added to the *Book of Order*:

> Those who are called to office in the church are to lead a life in obedience to Scripture and in conformity to the historic standards of the church. Among these standards is the requirement to live either in fidelity within the covenant of marriage between a man and a woman (W-4.9001), or chastity in singleness. Persons refusing to repent of any self-acknowledged practice, which the confessions call sin, shall not be ordained and/or installed as deacons, elders or ministers of the Word and Sacrament. (G-6.0106b in the old Form of Government)

The 2006 General Assembly, acting on a recommendation from its special Task Force on the Peace, Unity and Purity of the Church—and recalling a tradition dating back to the Adopting Act of 1729—declared that sessions or presbyteries may allow candidates to declare certain "scruples" with which they disagree. If the ordaining council judges those scrupled teachings to be nonessential, it may proceed with ordination anyway. The next General Assembly, in 2008, went further, revoking all previous "interpretive statements concerning ordained service of homosexual church members."

The "fidelity and chastity" paragraph, however, remained in the *Constitution*. The next General Assembly, in 2010, approved the present Form of Government and sent it to the presbyteries for their affirmative or negative vote. Included in that draft document was the "fidelity and chastity" language from the old book (the General Assembly insisted that it be included, so as not to tie the fate of the new Form of Government to that single paragraph). An additional proposed amendment directed that the paragraph be replaced by another.

Both amendments passed the presbyteries. The result is G-2.0104, a description of "gifts and qualities for ordained office":

a. To those called to exercise special functions in the church—deacons, ruling elders, and teaching elders—God gives suitable gifts for their various duties. In addition to possessing the necessary gifts and abilities, those who undertake particular ministries should be persons of strong faith, dedicated discipleship, and love of Jesus Christ as Savior and Lord. Their manner of life should be a demonstration of the Christian gospel in the church and in the world. They must have the approval of God's people and the concurring judgment of a council of the church.

b. Standards for ordained service reflect the church's desire to submit joyfully to the Lordship of Jesus Christ in all aspects of life (F-1.02). The council responsible for ordination and/or installation (G-2.0402; G-2.0607; G-3.0306) shall examine each candidate's calling, gifts, preparation, and suitability for the responsibilities of ordered ministry. The examination shall include, but not be limited to, a determination of the candidate's ability and commitment to fulfill all requirements as expressed in the constitutional questions for ordination and installation (W-4.4003). Councils shall be guided by Scripture and the confessions in applying standards to individual candidates.

The crux of the issue is how the phrase "manner of life" is to be interpreted. The *Book of Order* is clear that ordaining councils—who, ideally, know the candidates best—are to make such decisions on a case-by-case basis, "guided by Scripture and the confessions in applying standards to individual candidates."

While some have derided the silence of the present ordination standards on matters of sexual ethics as "local option" thinking—or even "presbygationalism"—that characterization is not historically accurate. Such constitutional specificity is relatively unusual in Presbyterian history, belonging to the relatively brief period from 1998 to 2011. Through most of its history—and again, in the present day—the Presbyterian Church's prevailing practice has been to rely on local ordaining councils to interpret the *Constitution*'s general standards.

Deacons

Of the three Reformed orders of ministry, that of deacon has the clearest, most unambiguous scriptural warrant. Acts 6:1–6 tells of the precise moment in history when the diaconate was established, a detail that cannot be discerned in the case of ruling and teaching elders.

The diaconate has its origin, literally, in a food fight—not the sort that phrase typically calls to mind, but a disagreement over policies governing the distribution of food to the needy. During a time of rapid growth in the church, "the Hellenists complained against the Hebrews because their widows were being neglected in the daily distribution of food" (Acts 6:1). That sentence is rich in historical context. Not only does it highlight the deep fault line in the early church—so evident in the letters of Paul—between Christians who came out of the Jewish tradition and newer converts from the Greek city-states. It also reveals that a principal activity of the early church was social-welfare work.

That, historians are coming to appreciate, is one of the hallmarks of the early Christian church and a principal explanation for its rapid growth throughout the Roman world. One of the first people to make this observation was Tertullian, around 200 CE. He quotes his fellow Romans, who by that time had come to say of their Christian neighbors, with great admiration, "See, how they love one another!" (*Apology*, 39.7). Tertullian is not talking about a friendly embrace during the passing of the peace. He is describing how Christians broke out of the prevailing Roman understanding of virtue.

Ancient Roman morality praised altruism up to, but usually not beyond, the limits of one's own extended family. To most of Roman culture, kinship was everything. The practice of maintaining a community feeding program for needy widows and orphans was inconceivable. Yet this was exactly what the early Christian church did. The people who made this sort of social ministry happen—therefore displaying to the world the unique nature of Christian agape—were the deacons.

Calvin too viewed the ministry of deacons as essential. Digging deep into the New Testament, he concluded that the order of ministry described in Acts 6 bore little resemblance to the medieval Roman Catholic diaconate. By Calvin's time, that office had lost its original meaning and had become a minor order—just one of a series of stepping stones on the road to priestly ordination. Ordination to the diaconate often took place on the same day as a man's ordination to the priesthood: a barely discernible nod to a long-disused order of ministry.

Calvin restored and transformed the ancient order, giving his deacons a major role in operating the sprawling ecclesiastical social-welfare system that cared for Geneva's poor and destitute. It was, in part, this compassionate witness of the city's charitable institutions that led Knox to famously describe Geneva as "the most perfect school of Christ that ever was in the earth since the days of the apostles."

By the time the Presbyterian diaconate made its way across the Atlantic, it had developed two separate but interrelated responsibilities. These are clearly seen in the following excerpt from the Presbyterian *Constitution* of 1788: "The Scriptures clearly point out deacons as distinct officers in the church, whose business it is to take care of the poor, and to distribute among them the collections which may be raised for their use. To them also may be properly committed the management of their temporal affairs in the church."[1]

The two responsibilities are care for the poor and stewardship of financial assets. These go hand in hand, because management of charitable funds is often necessary for social-welfare work. Yet the two are clearly not of equal importance. Even the *Constitution* of 1788 reflects this understanding, in using the permissive "may" to describe deacons' financial-oversight responsibilities. Not only that, it goes on to use the word "their" to refer to "temporal affairs." What is meant here is designated deacons' funds, not the funds of the entire church.

There have been times in American Presbyterian history when the two responsibilities of deacons have become inverted in importance. In some parts of the church, boards of deacons functioned as little more than financial trustee boards, exercising no responsibility for social welfare beyond monitoring budgeted expenditures.

One of the leading recommendations of the 1982 World Council of Churches' *Baptism, Eucharist and Ministry* consensus document is that the biblical order of deacon deserves to be reinvigorated, with servanthood forming the heart of such renewal efforts. The Presbyterian Church (U.S.A.) Task Force on the Theology and Practice of Ordination, in its report to the General Assembly ten years later, echoes that recommendation.[2] It goes on to recommend that deacons have a visible role in the church's worship—emphasizing particularly the reading of Scripture, the presentation of the gifts of the people, and assisting in serving the sacrament of the Lord's Supper. This last duty recalls the ancient task of waiting on tables.

The servant role is clearly seen in the *Book of Order*'s description of deacons' ministry as "one of compassion, witness, and service, sharing in the redeeming love of Jesus Christ for the poor, the hungry, the sick, the lost, the friendless, the oppressed, those burdened by unjust policies or structures, or anyone in distress" (G-2.0201). Other than organizing their own ministries of compassion, deacons typically have no other decision-making authority in the life of the church. They perform their duties under the oversight of the session (G-2.0202).

The *Book of Order* does note that among the tasks sessions may delegate to deacons is "overseeing the buildings and property of the congregation."

1. *The Constitution of the Presbyterian Church in the United States of America* (Philadelphia: Thomas Bradford, 1789), v.
2. Presbyterian Church (U.S.A.), *A Proposal for Considering the Theology and Practice of Ordination to Office in the Presbyterian Church (U.S.A.)* (Louisville, KY: Theology and Worship Ministry Unit, 1992).

It should be noted that this potential responsibility comes dead last in the long list of deacons' responsibilities. Clearly, a board of deacons that focuses on financial management to the exclusion of direct ministries of "compassion, witness, and service" is neglecting the greater portion of its biblical responsibilities.

G-2.0202 allows for the possibility that congregations may vote not to utilize the order of deacon. It also allows that deacons may not only be organized as a board, but may also be individually commissioned. In congregations that do not use the order of deacon, "the function of this ordered ministry shall be the responsibility of the ruling elders and the session" (G-2.0202).

As is the case with ruling elders, those elected by the congregation to serve as deacons must first undergo a period of study, after which the session "shall examine them as to their personal faith; knowledge of the doctrine, government, and discipline contained in the Constitution of the church; and the duties of the ministry," as well as determining that they are willing to serve (G-2.0402). Following this concurring vote, the newly elected deacons are ordained in a service of worship.

Ruling Elders

Those seeking to understand the role of ruling elders in the Presbyterian Church are immediately faced with a linguistic challenge. As the English language has evolved, the modifier "ruling" has almost completely lost its original meaning. To modern ears, the verb "to rule" evokes the work of a monarch, or perhaps the judge of a high court. Kings and queens rule over their subjects. Judges issue definitive rulings that constrain the behavior of others. Presbyterian elders rule in a very different sense.

Imagine an old-fashioned fabric store. Customers walk up and down among the colorful bolts of fabric displayed on the shelves. Making their selections, they bring them to the sales counter. Indicating the number of yards they wish to purchase, customers rely on the store clerks to cut off the appropriate length of material with a large set of shears. How do the clerks manage to do so accurately, with bolt after bolt of fabric? How do they manage not only to dispense the cotton or linen in increments of exactly one yard, but also to cut the fabric in a straight line, every time?

They utilize a trick of the fabric seller's trade. Attached to the edge of the sales counter is a ruler, precisely one yard in length. This is what they use to measure the fabric. When it comes time to make the cut, they run the scissors along this straight edge, guaranteeing that the hand that holds the shears does not waver.

This is like the function of ruling elders in the church. Every congregation needs a straight-edge ruler, permanently installed. Both in discerning future directions for the congregation and in overseeing the spiritual lives of the flock, the session is that ruler. The standard measure that ruling elders apply to the work of congregational governance is not a strip of steel with thirty-six notches, but rather the historic standards of Scripture and Confessions.

There is peril in assigning such responsibility to fallible individuals. This is why Presbyterian polity assigns it only to groups: to sessions at the congregational level, and to presbytery, synods, and the General Assembly at higher levels. Imagine if the clerk in the fabric store were to boast: "I need no ruler! My eye is so good, I always measure out exactly thirty-six inches. My hand is so steady, I never fail to cut a straight line." Customers in such an establishment would have good reason to suspect they were not getting value for money.

While the *Book of Order* describes certain personal characteristics ruling elders ought to display as spiritual leaders and exemplars, it also lays out all their ruling responsibilities in collective terms, as belonging to the session. "Congregations," G-2.0301 instructs, "should elect persons of wisdom and maturity of faith, having demonstrated skills in leadership and being compassionate in spirit." Those are the individual gifts ruling elders are expected to bring to their service to the church. Collectively—along with the teaching elders who also serve with them on the session—they "exercise leadership, government, spiritual discernment, and discipline and have responsibilities for the life of a congregation as well as the whole church, including ecumenical relationships."

The *Book of Order*'s definition of ruling elder gives voice to another important principle of Presbyterian governance: that of parity between ruling elders and teaching elders. G-2.0301 concludes by saying: "When elected as commissioners to higher councils, ruling elders participate and vote with the same authority as teaching elders, and they are eligible for any office."

Commissioned and Certified Service

Ruling elders are also eligible, with additional training, to be deployed as pastors of congregations on a temporary basis. Such individuals are known as Commissioned Ruling Elders—or, more precisely, Ruling Elders Commissioned to Particular Pastoral Service (formerly known as Commissioned Lay Preachers). Most often, presbyteries use these individuals to meet the needs of smaller congregations who would not otherwise receive pastoral services.

The services offered by Commissioned Ruling Elders are both limited and temporary. They are restricted to the particular congregation to which the presbytery appoints them, and they last for a limited period of time: a renewable three-year term, reviewed annually (G-2.1001). Commissioned Ruling Elders may be authorized to celebrate the sacraments and to preside at marriage ceremonies, if state law allows it. A teaching elder must work closely with the Commissioned Ruling Elder as "a mentor and supervisor" (G-2.1004).

The *Book of Order* also contains provisions for "Certified Church Service." Christian educators originally inspired the creation of this category of service, which has since been expanded to allow for the possibility of other sorts of professional certification (musicians, business administrators, and others), as long as a national certifying body for each specialized category of service is established under the oversight of the General Assembly.

Teaching Elders

While "teaching elder" is the *Book of Order*'s term of choice for those who preach and celebrate the sacraments, in G-2.0501 it introduces an alternate name for this order of ministry: "minister of the Word and Sacrament." Prior to the adoption of the present Form of Government, "minister of the Word and Sacrament"—or, colloquially, "minister"—was the standard term, and continues to be for most Reformed churches around the world. As we have said in the introduction, while "teaching elder" offers the advantage of clearly displaying the parity between the two varieties of presbyter (ruling and teaching) in Presbyterian governance, "minister of the Word and Sacrament" is more descriptive of the full range of functions performed by those who serve the church in this order of ministry.

Four principal functions—preaching/teaching, celebrating the sacraments, pastoral care, and governance—are identified as belonging to this order of ministry:

> When they serve as preachers and teachers of the Word, they shall preach and teach the faith of the church, so that the people are shaped by the pattern of the gospel and strengthened for witness and service. When they serve at font and table, they shall interpret the mysteries of grace and lift the people's vision toward the hope of God's new creation. When they serve as pastors, they shall support the people

Two verses from Scripture cited in this section are foundational to understanding the nature of this order of ministry. The first is Ephesians 4:12, which challenges teaching elders "to equip the saints for the work of ministry, for building up the body of Christ." The second, Jeremiah 3:15, is found in a footnote to the word "pastors": "I will give you shepherds after my own heart, who will feed you with knowledge and understanding."

in the disciplines of the faith amid the struggles of daily life. When they serve as presbyters, they shall participate in the responsibilities of governance, seeking always to discern the mind of Christ and to build up Christ's body through devotion, debate, and decision. (G-2.0501)

Teaching elders are not members of local congregations, although pastors and associate pastors are members of their church's session (G-3.0201). Rather, teaching elders are members of the presbytery. Calls to installed pastors or associate pastors are three-party covenants, involving pastors, sessions, and the presbytery, with pastors accountable to the presbytery, in conversation with the session. The terms of call cannot be changed, nor the call terminated, without the concurrence of the presbytery. Teaching elders serving in specialized ministries have accountability to the leadership of the ministry organization for which they labor, but they also remain accountable to the presbytery with respect to their overall life and ministry.

The Work of the Pastor

Setting aside for a moment the service of teaching elders in specialized ministries (whose relationship with the presbytery will be considered at greater length below, under the sixth Historic Principle, "Election by the People"), it is fitting to spend some time examining the normative work for teaching elders: pastoral ministry. Those who serve congregations as pastor, co-pastor, or associate pastor have these individual responsibilities: "They are to be responsible for a quality of life and relationships that commends the gospel to all persons and that communicates its joy and justice. They are responsible for studying, teaching, and preaching the Word, for celebrating Baptism and the Lord's Supper, and for praying with and for the congregation" (G-2.0504).

The first sentence makes it clear how very personal pastoral ministry is. Philips Brooks, in a famous turn of phrase from his landmark 1877 Lyman Beecher Lectures at Yale University, describes preaching as "the communication of truth through personality." It is not much of a stretch to extend his concept to all of pastoral ministry. Beecher argues that it is impossible to separate the person of the pastor from the work of ministry. An archaic word for parish minister is "parson," a word closely related to "person." The parson is literally God's person in a particular community.

Congregations depend on their pastors to spend time in prayer and study on their behalf. There is little enough opportunity for typical Christians to practice spiritual discernment in the workaday world, so to a certain degree they depend on their pastors to do it for them, then to ascend the pulpit and share what they have learned. The most faithful and effective pastors are those who resist the impulse of a success-driven society to transform themselves into pastoral administrators, pastoral counselors, pastoral entrepreneurs, pastoral recreation directors, pastoral fund-raisers, and all the rest, in favor of remaining plain-vanilla pastors: shepherds of the flock, God's person at the beating heart of the community.

The pastor's lifestyle "commends the gospel to all persons and . . . communicates its joy and justice." The pairing of joy and justice is a paradox. One is light; the other is ponderous. One is uplifting; the other is grounding. One is a colorful, hot-air balloon, soaring into the heavens; the other is the Supreme Court building, solemnly squatting upon its plinth of cold marble. One conveys happiness; the other whispers a vague sense of dread, evoking the awful price divine justice will demand on the day when it is truly loosed upon the earth.

Paradoxes such as these are pastors' stock in trade. Teaching elders hold them lightly, like a thistle. They examine them, not fully understanding their every nuance. In God's time, they communicate them, setting them loose to spread like holy contagion.

The activities by which pastors accomplish such purposes are listed next: "studying, teaching, and preaching the Word . . . celebrating Baptism and the Lord's Supper . . . praying with and for the congregation." Word. Sacrament. Prayer. Worship. None of these pastoral to-do-list items tops the glitzy church-growth consultant's agenda for how to market a congregation. They are the staples, the essentials. In the end, they are the only pastoral activities that truly matter.

The *Book of Order* next lists some tasks pastors are meant to do, in concert with the ruling elders and deacons of the congregation:

> With the ruling elders, they are to encourage people in the worship and service of God; to equip and enable them for their tasks within the church and their mission in the world; to exercise pastoral care, devoting special attention to the poor, the sick, the troubled, and the dying; to participate in governing responsibilities, including leadership of the congregation in implementing the principles of participation and inclusiveness in the decision-making life of the congregation, and its task of reaching out in concern and service to the life of the human community as a whole. With the deacons they are to share in the ministries of compassion, witness, and service. In addition to these pastoral duties, they are responsible for sharing in the ministry of the church in councils higher than the session and in ecumenical relationships. (G-2.0504)

Such an extensive list can generate enough anxiety to cause any sensible person to lose sleep at night. The good news is, there is no need for pastors to attack every item on this nightmarish to-do list alone. These tasks belong, collectively, to all the ordained leaders of the church. Once they have finished their commending and communicating, pastors join the deacons and ruling elders in discerning the best place to start working on that imposing list, trusting God to take it from there.

This is a great advantage of the Presbyterian concept of ministry: there is always plenty of help—at least, in theory. The more pastors persist in helping their congregations realize the Reformers' vision, following the thread of Presbyterian DNA that runs clean through the *Book of Order* from beginning to end, the more likely they are to behold their congregations rise up and move from hopeful theory to holy practice.

Installed Pastoral Relationships

One of the features of the former *Book of Order* that caused it to swell to such an unwieldy size was its extensive treatment of pastoral relationships. Chapter 14 of that book, a Pharisee's treasure trove of rules and regulations governing pastoral ministry, had absorbed a multitude of amendments over the years. Some regarded that chapter as like the proverbial bicycle inner tube that has been patched so many times, no one could guess how much original rubber remained.

Wisely, when it came to the complex subject of pastoral relationships, the authors of the present Form of Government decided to tear off all the patches and start afresh. The present book offers considerable flexibility for presbyteries to work out their own guidelines for establishing teaching elders in pastoral service. Presbyteries who wish to continue the old, higher level of regulatory detail are free to do so, defining such policies in their manual of operations.

The three installed pastoral relationships are unchanged: pastor, associate pastor, and co-pastor (G-2.0504a). The temporary position from the old Form of Government formerly known as designated pastor is now included here, among the installed positions, as a variation on how pastors

---

The relatively uncommon position of co-pastor was conceived as an alternative, nonhierarchical configuration for congregations with more than one teaching elder. In a co-pastor arrangement, one or more pastors interact as colleagues in an egalitarian fashion rather than as pastor/head of staff and associate. Co-pastor arrangements are rare, because they require a high degree of compatibility between or among the teaching elders sharing pastoral duties. Should one of the co-pastors depart, it can be difficult to replicate the unique synchronicity of skills the founding partners enjoyed. The most enduring co-pastor arrangements have proven to be those between two teaching elders who are married to one another.

may be called. This designated term provision makes it possible for presbyteries, in special cases and in consultation with the congregation, to approve the calls of pastors, associate pastors, or co-pastors for a limited, renewable term, thereby sparing struggling congregations a protracted pastoral transition. Those in designated positions are eligible to be considered for a permanent position in the future, if all three parties (teaching elder, congregation, and presbytery) remain agreeable.

Because associate pastors are called by the congregation, through the presbytery, they are not expected automatically to resign when the pastor departs from the congregation or when a new one arrives (G-2.0504a). In larger congregations, associates often provide valued continuity and steady leadership during the instability of the interim period. When the new installed pastor arrives, all parties should commit to a season of mutual discernment in which responsibilities are renegotiated and job descriptions amended to reflect the new mix of talents and spiritual gifts present on the staff. If a renewed and redefined working relationship is the result, that is to be celebrated. If, on the other hand, changed circumstances lead an associate to seek a new call elsewhere, that in no way reflects badly upon the associate. In such a case, the session and presbytery should do everything they can to ease the transition.

It is wrong for newly called pastors to assume, as a matter of policy, that "the decks will be cleared," with incumbent associate pastors submitting resignations upon their arrival, for the new pastor to accept or hand back. It is equally wrong for associates to assume their duties will continue exactly as they were before the transition. Every pastoral transition in multiple-staff churches is unique. The details must be worked out on a case-by-case basis.

One thing is clear, however: it is seldom the case that associate pastors ought to be called as pastors of the congregation they are presently serving. The *Book of Order*—faithful to its preference for fostering flexibility and decision making on the local level—stops short of an outright prohibition, as was the case in previous editions (G-2.0504a). Yet the warning that "an associate pastor is ordinarily not eligible to be the next installed pastor of that congregation" ought to be taken very seriously indeed. That admonition grows out of decades of experience with all manner of churches, resulting in the conclusion that associate-to-pastor transitions seldom turn out well.

While presbyteries have ultimate authority over the work of associate pastors, typically they delegate much of that authority to designated individuals or groups on the congregational level. In nearly every case this is the pastor, serving as head of staff, in conversation with a personnel committee of the session. It is of crucial importance that expectations of accountability for associate pastors be clearly negotiated before work

The *Book of Order* has never addressed the subject of staff relationships in churches served by one or more teaching elders. The titles "senior pastor" and "head of staff" do not occur at all, nor do specialist designations such as "youth pastor," "executive pastor," "mission pastor," and the like—even though they are in common usage in many larger congregations. The details of such cooperative working arrangements are left to the session to determine and to present to the presbytery for approval (G-2.0504b).

begins and that they be spelled out in job descriptions, personnel policy manuals, and similar documents, so there is no ambiguity. Vague or undefined expectations are the enemy of harmony on a church staff.

Sessions and pastors serving as heads of staff need carefully to protect their associates' right to access the presbytery's committee on ministry (or comparable group) as they navigate the sometimes-rough waters of staff relationships. The *Book of Order* clearly says: "In the performance of that ministry, the teaching elder shall be accountable to the presbytery" (G-2.0502). It specifies no different accountability procedures for associate pastors.

Associate pastors must exercise prudence in pursuing this avenue, understanding that the pastor, as head of staff, is acting as an agent of the presbytery in supervising their day-to-day work. That means presbyteries ordinarily expect associates to share concerns directly with the pastor first. If, after exhausting such ordinary avenues, associates feel they still need to speak with a member of the committee on ministry, that is their right.

Another possible resource is the session's personnel committee (or a similar committee having oversight of personnel matters). Wise pastors recruit experienced ruling elders to serve on this key committee, people who have much to contribute toward resolving difficulties that arise on a church staff.

The word "collegiality" is commonly held up as a virtue on church staffs. The word has a variety of meanings. On one end of the spectrum of meaning, it refers to something like the relationship between co-pastors: two people sharing work responsibilities as equal partners, working out differences through mutual negotiation. At the other end of the spectrum, it means a congenial and cooperative working relationship built on the recognition that one of the partners exercises supervisory responsibilities over the other. In most cases of pastors and associate pastors successfully working together, the truth is closer to the supervisory end of the spectrum. Pastors do typically exercise a supervisory relationship over associate pastors; otherwise, both positions would be called co-pastor. While it

Members of local personnel committees or presbytery committees on ministry should remain alert to signs of triangulation. This is a process whereby the healthy functioning of a two-party relationship is subverted by the introduction of relationships with one or more additional parties. For example, in a conflict situation one combatant may ask a committee member to convey messages to the other party. This is rarely effective. It is better to coach both parties on how to communicate more effectively with each other.

is true that both pastors and associates are called by the congregation, this does not put them on an equal footing with respect to supervision. The fact that the congregation has voted to call one position "pastor" and the other "associate pastor" implies that the congregation wants the pastor to supervise the work of the associate.

It is the responsibility of pastors to take the lead role in maintaining the collegial character of the mutual working relationship. The ordinary human dynamics of such situations being what they are, it is easier for the supervisor to foster and encourage collegiality than for the person being supervised successfully to demand it. The strongest, most mutually supportive staff relationships are the most collegial ones, and collegiality is largely a product of pastors feeling comfortable enough in their own skin to delegate a variety of important tasks to associates without seeking to micromanage their work. Pastors who do not allow for a zone of independent decision making within the boundaries of the associate's defined duties fail in their responsibilities as heads of staff.

Temporary Pastoral Relationships
The *Book of Order* combines the several temporary pastoral relationships that have become familiar from earlier editions of the book—interim pastors, stated supply pastors, and temporary supply pastors—into a single category: "temporary pastoral relationships" (G-2.0504b). The same guidelines now govern them all. Assignments to temporary pastoral positions are made for no longer than one year at a time. Those holding temporary positions are "ordinarily not eligible to serve as the next installed pastor, co-pastor, or associate pastor" of that congregation, although occasional exceptions may be made by three-fourths of those present and voting in a presbytery meeting (G-2.0504c).

In keeping with the *Book of Order*'s general tendency toward simplification and its preference for allowing polity solutions to be worked out locally, presbyteries are free to continue utilizing the former titles and types of temporary relationships if they wish. Alternatively, presbyteries are free to create new types of temporary positions of their own devising or to combine them under a single "Temporary Pastor" title. Whichever temporary categories a presbytery decides to use on a regular basis should be detailed in the presbytery's manual of operations.

Because the titles of the former temporary positions remain in general use in many presbyteries, it is worthwhile becoming familiar with the traditional characteristics of each one. There is some overlap in function among them.

Interim pastors serve congregations during the time of vacancy between pastors. Typically these are teaching elders of long experience who have received specialized training to shepherd congregations through this difficult transitional period, which lasts between one and two years on the average. This allows the pastor nominating committee time to do its job thoroughly and deliberately, without feeling undue pressure from the congregation to rush the process. Most interim pastors bring specialized knowledge of organizational dynamics and conflict management. In agreeing to accept the interim position, they pledge not to become a candidate for the installed-pastor position. While interim pastors usually moderate the session during their tenure, they agree not to advise the pastor nominating committee concerning their work (such counsel is typically provided by a committee of the presbytery). Some interim pastors serve primarily within a given geographic area. Others are highly mobile, moving freely throughout the denomination, changing their presbytery membership frequently.

Stated supply pastors are appointed by the presbytery to preach and lead worship in congregations that are not ready to search for an installed pastor. Often these are part-time assignments to small churches that offer few programs or activities other than a weekly worship service. While listed as temporary positions, some stated-supply arrangements continue for many years, renewed annually. Many stated-supply positions are part-time and are filled by honorably retired teaching elders, "tentmaking" teaching elders (those who have other paid employment), or commissioned ruling elders (G-2.10).

Temporary supply is a loosely defined category covering every other type of temporary pastoral service, including week-by-week pulpit supply arrangements, service performed by seminary students as part of their field education, covering a pastor's absence due to temporary disability or sabbatical leave, and similar needs.

Chapter 8

TRUTH AND GOODNESS

That truth is in order to goodness; and the great touchstone of truth, its tendency to promote holiness, according to our Savior's rule, "By their fruits ye shall know them." And that no opinion can either be more pernicious or more absurd than that which brings truth and falsehood upon a level, and represents it as of no consequence what a man's opinions are. On the contrary, we are persuaded that there is an inseparable connection between faith and practice, truth and duty. Otherwise it would be of no consequence either to discover truth or to embrace it. (F-3.0104)

"Truth is in order to goodness" is an obscure eighteenth-century expression that begs for translation into contemporary language. The simplest explanation is that truth and goodness are inseparably linked together. They participate in the same reality. They are twins.

Truth and goodness are twins. According to many philosophical tenets of our present age, that statement is nonsense—or, at the very least, wishful thinking. To the most recent generation of skeptics, there is no such thing as absolute moral goodness. There are only individual, relative goods.

Others maintain that truth—especially scientific truth—does have absolute existence, quite apart from any moral goodness. The truths revealed in the laboratory and the nuclear accelerator are value blind. According to the most positivistic of scientific worldviews, this thoroughly materialistic universe is hurtling toward a random goal that has no moral significance whatsoever. It's a jungle out there, and the law of the jungle—survival of the fittest—is the only constant.

There is scientific truth, and there is moral truth. The genius of Christianity—and particularly the Presbyterian expression of Christianity, which has such a high regard for education of every kind—is that it strives to marry the two.

Presbyterian polity takes a holistic approach when it comes to balancing

> Someone once asked Winston Churchill if he thought the Arthurian legend is true. "I don't know," replied the prime minister. "But if it's not, it should be."

77

truth and goodness. "The great touchstone of truth [is] its tendency to promote holiness." Those who are holy are set apart to participate in the reality of God. Because God is the author of truth, those who devote themselves to pursuing it are participating in a holy task. "I am the way, and the truth, and the life," says our Lord (John 14:6). "You will know the truth, and the truth will make you free" (John 8:32).

Truth Matters

The fourth Historic Principle maintains that "no opinion can either be more pernicious or more absurd than that which brings truth and falsehood upon a level, and represents it as of no consequence what a man's opinions are." Truly, these are words for our times. Earlier generations worried about moral relativism. To that concern is added, in our day, the new scourge of informational relativism.

The Internet offers a chaotic, surging sea of information. Hypertext technology allows the naive, the careless, and the gullible to surf at will, paying scant attention to foundational sources and documentation. Enterprising bloggers claim lordship over scholarly domains entirely of their own creation. In the brave new online world of disconnected ideas, long-established authorities compete with brash newcomers on a seemingly equal footing. In the eyes of many, truth is whatever one chooses

---

Marva Dawn tells a chilling story of a conversation she had with a young woman at a Christian youth convention:

> She asked me what I thought about a certain matter of sexual ethics. I answered her with the most careful biblical reading and ethical nuancing I had gained in years of training.
>
> She responded, "Well, I just wanted to know your opinion."
>
> "That wasn't my opinion," I replied. "If I had given you my opinion, it would have been the opposite, because I really would like to escape these biblical truths and say what pleases everybody. I tried to tell you as faithfully as I could what all my studies have discerned God is saying. That's much more sound, more reliable, more eternally true than my measly opinion."
>
> She looked at me in shock. How could anyone question the importance of personal opinion? How could anyone give an answer different from her own private feelings? Is there really such a thing as public truth?
>
> Yes there is. And truth's name is God. (Marva Dawn, *Talking the Walk: Letting Christian Language Live Again* (Grand Rapids: Brazos Press, 2005), 83.)

to assert—and the louder, the better. Sow the seeds of your own personal truth on social media, harvest thousands of "likes," and watch the stodgy traditional authorities fight to stay afloat in the ensuing deluge.

The Westminster Larger Catechism offers a detailed exposition of the Ten Commandments. This confession is remarkable in portraying the commandments not only in negative fashion—the proverbial "Thou shalt nots"—but also as a source of positive instruction. Discussing the Ninth Commandment, against lying, the Larger Catechism flips the topic into the realm of the positive, cataloging the characteristics of a person who loves the truth:

> The duties required in the Ninth Commandment are: the preserving and promoting of truth between man and man, and the good name of our neighbor, as well as our own; appearing and standing for the truth; and from the heart, sincerely, freely, clearly, and fully, speaking the truth, and only the truth, in matters of judgment and justice, and in all other things whatsoever; a charitable esteem of our neighbors, loving, desiring, and rejoicing in their good name; sorrowing for, and covering of their infirmities; freely acknowledging of their gifts and graces, defending their innocency; a ready receiving of good report, and unwillingness to admit of an evil report concerning them; discouraging talebearers, flatterers, and slanderers; love and care of our own good name, and defending it when need requireth; keeping of lawful promises; studying and practicing of whatsoever things are true, honest, lovely, and of good report. (7.254)

According to the Second Helvetic Confession, the very purpose of the church—and the reason it has persisted throughout its long history and will continue to persist—is to lead people to the truth:

> THE CHURCH HAS ALWAYS EXISTED AND IT WILL ALWAYS EXIST. But because God from the beginning would have men to be saved, and to come to the knowledge of the truth (I Tim. 2:4), it is altogether necessary that there always should have been, and should be now, and to the end of the world, a Church. (5.124)

"Knowledge of the truth" cannot always be defined with absolute precision. Such is the hard-won understanding of the Presbyterian Church (U.S.A.) after casting off the intellectual shackles of fundamentalism in the early twentieth century.

Those ordained to serve the church in ordered ministries swear to "receive and adopt the essential tenets of the Reformed faith as expressed in the confessions of our church" (W-4.4003c). In an earlier time, such a statement would have been understood to mean subscription to every word of a confessional document such as the Westminster Confession.

Beginning with the Adopting Act of 1729 (by which the Synod of Philadelphia made room for those unwilling to subscribe to certain chapters of the Westminster Confession by permitting them to declare "scruples"), through the General Assembly's 1927 adoption of the report of the Swearingen Commission (assigning ultimate authority to presbyteries to determine candidates' adherence to the "essential tenets"), the church has made room for a certain amount of theological diversity.

> The portions of the Westminster Confession most often scrupled (or waived as an ordination requirement) in the eighteenth century were chapters XX ("Of Christian Liberty, and Liberty of Conscience") and XXIII ("Of the Civil Magistrate"). These are the passages supporting the divine right of kings.

Periodically, the General Assembly receives overtures from presbyteries seeking greater precision, asking for a checklist of essential tenets (or beliefs) that can be used in examining candidates. That is precisely what the "Five Fundamentals" that gave fundamentalism its name were. Whenever the Assembly has received such a request in modern times, it has refused it, declaring that the *Constitution* of the church—particularly the *Book of Confessions*—is adequate for that purpose.

The Five Fundamentals are (1) the inerrancy of inspired Scripture, (2) the historical reality of the virgin birth of Jesus, (3) the substitutionary doctrine of Christ's atonement for sin, (4) the bodily resurrection of Jesus, and (5) the historical reality of Jesus' miracles. The question that must be asked of this list is whether it is truly fundamental—a compilation of the most essential proclamations of Christianity—or whether it is merely a list of hotbutton issues that had arisen in theological debates of the time, in response to biblical higher criticism and certain scientific discoveries.

There are portions of the Foundations section of the *Book of Order* that come close to filling that bill—but not completely. F-2.03, "The Confessions as Statements of the Faith of the Church Catholic," for example, gives special mention to the doctrines of the Trinity and the incarnation: "the ecumenical creeds, notably the Nicene and Apostles' Creeds with their definitions of the mystery of the triune God and of the incarnation of the eternal Word of God in Jesus Christ."

F-2.04, "The Confessions as Statements of the Faith of the Protestant Reformation," mentions "God's grace in Jesus Christ as revealed in the Scriptures" and "the Protestant watchwords—grace alone, faith alone, Scripture alone" as essential doctrines of the Reformation.

F-2.05, "The Confessions as Statements of the Faith of the Reformed Tradition," contains the following list:

The election of the people of God for service as well as for
salvation;

Covenant life marked by a disciplined concern for order
in the church according to the Word of God;

A faithful stewardship that shuns ostentation and seeks
proper use of the gifts of God's creation; and

The recognition of the human tendency to idolatry and
tyranny, which calls the people of God to work for the
transformation of society by seeking justice and living
in obedience to the Word of God.

These limited lists point presbyteries and sessions in the direction of
a broad doctrinal consensus at the heart of Presbyterianism, but none of
them rises to the level of a comprehensive declaration of essential tenets.
Ultimately, section G-2.0104b of the Form of Government leaves the decision up to the ordaining body:

The council responsible for ordination and/or installation (G-2.0402;
G-2.0607; G-3.0306) shall examine each candidate's calling, gifts,
preparation, and suitability for the responsibilities of ordered ministry. The examination shall include, but not be limited to, a determination of the candidate's ability and commitment to fulfill all
requirements as expressed in the constitutional questions for ordination and installation (W-4.4003). Councils shall be guided by
Scripture and the confessions in applying standards to individual
candidates.

Presbyterians value the use of reason in pursuing the truth, but reason
goes only so far. The greatest truths of this life are revealed truths. Perhaps
only the poets can truly explain this limitation of the human condition, as
William Butler Yeats once observed in his diary: "We taste and feel and see
the truth. We do not reason ourselves into it."

Goodness Matters

Presbyterians minister in a culture that is double minded with respect
to the existence of absolute moral goodness. On the one hand, there is
a tendency to deny the reality of sin and celebrate goodness so broadly
that it loses nearly all meaning. "I believe everyone is basically good" is
a common-enough creed—willfully avoiding realities such as the Nazi
Holocaust, the sexual abuse of children, the scourge of terrorism, and the
ease with which greed corrupts politics.

On the other hand, there is a cynical tendency to deny the possibility of
any human progress toward the good. When public figures who have been

outspoken in pursuing the common good prove to be less than completely virtuous—witness the television preacher with the proverbial feet of clay—swift is their fall, and its report is echoed loudly and gleefully in the mass media. Recall, for example, the astonishing amount of coverage the news media gave to the release of Mother Teresa's private diaries, which portray her as only human in her grappling with the great questions of life.

In the Gospel of Luke, John the Baptist sends a few of his disciples on a scouting expedition to investigate whether or not Jesus truly is the Messiah. The emissaries decide simply to ask him. The answer Jesus gives is oblique: "Go and tell John what you have seen and heard: the blind receive their sight, the lame walk, the lepers are cleansed, the deaf hear, the dead are raised, the poor have good news brought to them. And blessed is anyone who takes no offense at me" (Luke 7:22–23).

Our culture may be cynical about the existence of true goodness, but when it does encounter it in the wild, it can only accord it the respect it deserves. "By their fruits you shall know them" is what this fourth Historic Principle affirms.

Holiness Matters

The fruit of truth and goodness, according to the fourth Historic Principle, is holiness. The Reformed tradition regards with skepticism any claim that human beings may, by their own spiritual striving, attain personal holiness. We are not a "holiness church" in the Arminian tradition. Presbyterians understand sin to be so pervasive that it can never be wholly vanquished in this life.

Nevertheless, there is a place in Presbyterianism for sanctification. The Westminster Larger Catechism defines sanctification as "a work of God's grace, whereby [the elect] . . . are, in time . . . renewed in their whole [person] after the image of God (7.185).

The Confession of 1967 puts it in more contemporary terms, speaking not of sanctification but of "new life." New life in Christ can be successfully pursued only in community. That pursuit is a lifelong task, with many false starts, wrong turnings, and blind alleys. Mere humans cannot hope to reach the goal in this life, but that is no reason to abandon the journey:

> The new life takes shape in a community in which men know that God loves and accepts them in spite of what they are. They therefore accept themselves and love others, knowing that no man has any ground on which to stand, except God's grace.

> The new life does not release a man from conflict with unbelief, pride, lust, fear. He still has to struggle with disheartening difficulties and problems. Nevertheless, as he matures in love and faithfulness in his life with Christ, he lives in freedom and good cheer, bearing witness

on good days and evil days, confident that the new life is pleasing to God and helpful to others. (9.22-9.23)

The consequence is that character matters in the life of any Christian, but particularly in the lives of those in ordained service. The Foundations section of the *Book of Order* explains:

> Because in Christ the Church is holy, the Church, its members, and those in its ordered ministries strive to lead lives worthy of the Gospel we proclaim. In gratitude for Christ's work of redemption, we rely upon the work of God's Spirit through Scripture and the means of grace (W-5.5001) to form every believer and every community for this holy living. We confess the persistence of sin in our corporate and individual lives. At the same time, we also confess that we are forgiven by Christ and called again and yet again to strive for the purity, righteousness, and truth revealed to us in Jesus Christ and promised to all people in God's new creation. (F-1.0302b)

Preaching, Teaching, and Christian Nurture

A hallmark of Presbyterianism is an emphasis on education as the search for truth. Calvin, Knox, and the other Reformers found inspiration in detailed study of the Scriptures in the original languages. Knowing how important it is that every Christian know the Scriptures, they worked to place vernacular translations of the Bible into every Presbyterian household.

In the earliest days of the American colonies, that educational tradition was expressed in William Tennent Sr.'s Log College, founded in Neshaminy, Pennsylvania—just northeast of Philadelphia—in 1726 or 1727. The exclusive purpose of this antecedent of both Princeton University and Princeton Theological Seminary was the training of pastors. Although their classroom was nothing more than a rudely constructed log cabin, Tennent's divinity students received instruction in Hebrew, Greek, and Latin, as well as theology and biblical studies. Their professor had no doctoral degree but was merely a pastor, trained at Edinburgh and ordained by the Presbyterian Church of Ireland. In that day and age, such an education offered sufficient preparation to gather a group of eager students and teach the basics of what a Presbyterian minister needed to know.

Today's ordination standards still require completion of courses in the biblical languages as well as a three-year postgraduate degree, followed by public examination. Those high standards are descended from this proud tradition of seeking God's truth in the Scriptures, empowered by education.

A significant feature of that tradition is the centrality of preaching, presented by those who have received sufficient training. We have already seen how "studying, teaching, and preaching the Word" are the very first pastoral responsibilities listed in G-2.0504. Among the general responsibilities of councils listed in G-3.0101, proclamation of the word comes first:

> Councils of the church exist to help congregations and the church as a whole to be more faithful participants in the mission of Christ. They do so as they
>
> > *Provide that the Word of God may be truly preached and heard,*
> > responding to the promise of God's new creation in Christ, and
> > inviting all people to participate in that new creation;
> > *Provide that the Sacraments may be rightly administered and received,*
> > welcoming those who are being engrafted into Christ,
> > bearing witness to Christ's saving death and resurrection,
> > anticipating the heavenly banquet that is to come, and
> > committing itself in the present to solidarity with the marginalized and the hungry; and
> > *Nurture a covenant community of disciples of Christ,*
> > living in the strength of God's promise, and
> > giving itself in service to God's mission.

The same is true of the responsibilities of sessions listed in G-3.0201a, which follow this same three-part outline. The first responsibility of the session is to

> *provide that the Word of God may be truly preached and heard.* This responsibility shall include providing a place where the congregation may regularly gather for worship, education, and spiritual nurture; providing for regular preaching of the Word by a teaching elder or other person prepared and approved for the work; planning and leading regular efforts to reach into the community and the world with the message of salvation and the invitation to enter into committed discipleship; planning and leading ministries of social healing and reconciliation in the community in accordance with the prophetic witness of Jesus Christ; and initiating and responding to ecumenical efforts that bear witness to the love and grace of God.

These responsibilities of sessions and pastors for overseeing the worship life of the congregation are further explained in W-1.4004 and W-1.4005.

The other two sets of session responsibilities—of equal importance—are to "provide that the Sacraments may be rightly administered and received" and to "nurture the covenant community of disciples of Christ."

It takes but little imagination to see that these responsibilities of sessions are structured around the three Reformed notes of the church: Word, sacrament, and discipline (F-1.0303).

The same is true of the responsibilities and powers of the presbytery enumerated in G-3.0301. The three-part structure of this section is similar to the one dealing with session responsibilities, although some of the particular responsibilities are different. The presbytery is primarily concerned to

> *provide that the Word of God may be truly preached and heard.* This responsibility shall include organizing, receiving, merging, dismissing, and dissolving congregations in consultation with their members; overseeing congregations without pastors; establishing pastoral relationships and dissolving them; guiding the preparation of those preparing to become teaching elders; establishing and maintaining those ecumenical relationships that will enlarge the life and mission of the church in its district; providing encouragement, guidance, and resources to congregations in the areas of mission, prophetic witness, leadership development, worship, evangelism, and responsible administration to the end that the church's witness to the love and grace of God may be heard in the world.

As with the session, other lists of responsibilities for the sacraments and for community life follow. Much the same is true for the responsibilities of synods (G-3.0401) and of the General Assembly (G-3.0501).

The Directory for Worship bears witness to the centrality of God's Word in Presbyterian worship:

The church confesses the Scriptures to be the Word of God written, witnessing to God's self-revelation. Where that Word is read and proclaimed, Jesus Christ the Living Word is present by the inward witness of the Holy Spirit. For this reason the reading, hearing, preaching, and confessing of the Word are central to Christian worship. The session shall ensure that in public worship the Scripture is read and proclaimed regularly in the common language(s) of the particular church. (W-2.2001)

'The *Book of Order* assigns particular responsibilities for proclaiming God's Word to teaching elders (or, when that is not possible, to specially trained ruling elders). In choosing Scripture texts for worship, for example, teaching elders "should exercise care so that over a period of time the people will hear the full message of Scripture" (W-2.2002). Lectionaries are commended (although optional) as a practical means of insuring that preachers venture further, in choosing Scripture passages, than their own personal canon of favorite selections (W-2.2003).

The public reading of Scripture is far from incidental to Presbyterian worship. Care should be taken to make sure God's people have ample opportunity to hear and understand it. The public reading of Scripture is a community enterprise, requiring not only preparation and skill on the part of the reader, but also a particular attitude of attentiveness in the listener: "The public reading of Scripture should be clear, audible, and attentive to the meanings of the text, and should be entrusted to those prepared for such reading. Listening to the reading of Scripture requires expectation and concentration and may be aided by the availability of a printed text for the worshipers" (W-2.2006).

Even more than the public reading of Scripture, the sermon interpreting it is the beating heart of Presbyterian worship. The language used here—in the tradition of the bold statement of the Second Helvetic Confession that "the preaching of the Word of God *is* the Word of God" (5.004)—identifies the sermon as a place where the congregation discerns the real presence of the risen and reigning Christ, just as they do in the sacraments (W-2.2007).

Sessions are also responsible for maintaining strong educational programs. Although this is briefly mentioned in the list of general session responsibilities, one of the most thorough and theologically grounded expressions of this responsibility is found in the Directory for Worship, W-6.2005. This section ties the session's educational responsibilities to the congregation's baptismal promises to nurture new believers in the faith:

> The session and the ruling elders are responsible for providing for the development and supervision of the educational program of the church, for instructing ruling elders and deacons, and for developing discipleship among members. (G-2.0301; G-3.201) The pastor nurtures the community through the ministries of Word and Sacrament, by praying with and for the congregation, through formal and informal teaching, and by example. (G-2.0104; G-2.0504) Some in the community of faith whose special gifts and training have prepared them for a ministry of education are called to the task of leadership in nurture. Teachers, advisers, and others appointed by the session guide, instruct, and equip those for whose education and nurture they are responsible. (W-3.3503)

All these responsibilities for preaching, teaching, and Christian nurture are grounded in the Reformed tradition's unshakable commitment to God's truth revealed in Jesus Christ and the bearing of that truth not only to God's people but to the entire world.

Chapter 9

MUTUAL FORBEARANCE

That, while under the conviction of the above principle we think it
necessary to make effectual provision that all who are admitted as
teachers be sound in the faith, we also believe that there are truths
and forms with respect to which men of good characters and
principles may differ. And in all these we think it the duty both
of private Christians and societies to exercise mutual forbearance
toward each other. (F-3.0105)

After offering their ringing declaration of the importance of truth telling,
the authors of the Historic Principles quickly follow it with a qualification:
"There are truths and forms with respect to which men of good characters
and principles may differ."

There are truths, and there are truths. Some are of a universal nature.
Others are of lesser importance. The key to getting along with others in
the church, when viewpoints differ on less consequential points, is *mutual
forbearance*.

"Forbearance" is an archaic term. Readers of the Authorized ("King
James") Version of the Bible can find it in Ephesians 4:2. In the face of
persistent church conflict, "forbearing one another in love, endeavoring to
keep the unity of the Spirit in the bond of peace" is the apostle's prescrip-
tion for good health in the body of Christ. The New Revised Standard
Version renders it "bearing with one another in love."

The essential feature of the biblical concept of mutual forbearance is the

---

One who was evidently familiar with mutual forbearance was the late
film star Robert Mitchum. A reporter once asked him to share the secret
of the success of his marriage of more than thirty years—an unheard-
of tenure in the divorce-friendly Hollywood culture. Mitchum's answer
was, "Mutual forbearance. We have each continued to believe the
other will do better tomorrow." The film star's marital credo recalls the
old bumper-sticker slogan: "Be patient: God isn't finished with me yet."

---

presence of a third party in the relationship: God. Whether the opposing parties are facing off across a kitchen table or a session conference table, two individuals in conflict have little chance of permanently resolving their differences until they have first acknowledged their mutual reliance on a higher authority. Such is the message of the Ephesians passage as it recommends "making every effort to maintain the unity of the Spirit in the bond of peace."

Note that unity in the relationship does not come from the parties themselves. It is unity *of the Spirit*. Further, the peace that reigns over the two opponents is not something that appears automatically, requiring little effort. The Scripture speaks of the "bond" of peace: literally, a chain or fetter. A lifelong commitment to peacemaking means sacrificing something of the freedom we would otherwise have, were we not accountable to another.

Dealing with Conflict

Although, as Paul's letters attest, conflict has been a feature of church life from the earliest days, the fantasy that complete harmony can be achieved in this fallen world is remarkably persistent. Christians tend to put inordinate energy into trying either to resolve or to suppress every conflict that arises within the body of Christ. We tend to fear anger, above all other emotions, as sinful and unchristian. As a consequence, when it becomes apparent that differences of opinion are not easily resolved, denial is too often the fallback position.

It is then that passive-aggressive behavior rears its sweetly smiling but ugly head. Passive-aggressive conflicts are waged in slow motion, through an intricately choreographed ritual dance. The principal rule of the dance is to deny the conflict's existence. The first one who allows anger to surface is considered the loser.

As a result, the conflict goes underground. Adversaries silently wage the battle beneath the outwardly serene surface of congregational life. The master warrior is the saboteur, the chief information officer the spy, the supply sergeant the gossip. The tactics are misdirection, delay, and outright inaction. The weapons are barbed comments, backhanded compliments, and the sniper-shot of "constructive criticism." Occasionally, one of the combatants—realizing the conflict is about to burst out publicly—takes evasive action: fomenting a smaller, seemingly unrelated conflict to deflect attention away from the true issue.

The fifth Historic Principle provides a viable alternative to the passive-aggressive approach to conflict: mutual forbearance. Solving disagreements is always preferable, but when that goal is not easily achieved, the next best choice is to name the conflict—perhaps wrapping some yellow warning tape around the perimeter—but to let it remain there in plain sight. The contending parties resolve to let congregational life continue to go on around it. Mutual forbearance is "agreeing to disagree."

Ecumenicity

Several themes we have already touched upon—laid out in the *Book of Order*'s foundational documents under the heading "Openness to the Guidance of the Holy Spirit" (F-1.04)—further highlight the importance of mutual forbearance.

The first, "Ecumenicity" (F-1.0402), speaks of forbearance on a larger scale than any single denomination—that of the ecumenical church: "The presbyterian system of government in the Constitution of the Presbyterian Church (U.S.A.) is established in light of Scripture but is not regarded as essential for the existence of the Christian Church nor required of all Christians."

In light of some of the denomination's past history—the excesses of which can only be described as Presbyterian triumphalism—this is an extraordinary statement. It declares, on the one hand, that Presbyterian church government is established on scriptural foundations. On the other, it admits that the Presbyterian interpretation of those Scriptures is not necessarily the only valid one. Presbyterian governance "is not regarded as essential," nor is it "required of all Christians."

This sort of thinking is an example of a highly useful theological principle from the days of the early Christian church. It occurs frequently in the Greek writings of theologians of the early centuries. It deserves to be better known today. The name of this concept is *adiaphora*. The Greek *diaphora* means "different." Adding the prefix *a-* makes it negative, so *adiaphora* means literally "no difference," or "it makes no difference."

What *adiaphora* means, in practical usage, is that a particular point of doctrine is nonessential. It is an issue that is important, yet not important enough to threaten the church's unity. A biblical example is Paul's discussion of the problem of food offered to idols in the letter to the Romans: "Those who eat must not despise those who abstain, and those who abstain must not pass judgment on those who eat; for God has welcomed them" (Rom. 14:3). Paul does not actually use the word *adiaphora* in this passage, but his advice to the Romans is clearly an example of the principle. In his eyes, there is no difference between vegetarians and omnivores when it comes to being a good Christian.

Adiaphora is a useful term for all sorts of church controversies, large or small. Pipe organ or electric guitar in worship? *Adiaphora*. Hymns or "praise songs"? *Adiaphora*. Pews or chairs in the sanctuary? *Adiaphora*. Tie and jacket or sport shirt on the male ruling elder or deacon serving communion? *Adiaphora*. Decisions do have to be made about such matters in the life of the church, but partisans on both sides need to understand the issue in proper perspective. If combatants can recognize that—win or lose—the decision need not threaten the church's essential unity, then the church's mission can go on, regardless of which side wins the vote. In a diverse society, and in an increasingly diverse Presbyterian Church, the ability to discern *adiaphora* is an essential tool for living together in community.

Nineteenth-century Presbyterian missionaries journeying to distant lands came to understand that many of the theological differences separating one Christian denomination from another were *adiaphora*. The fine points of disagreement separating one European theologian from another, several centuries after the original battle lines were drawn, meant little on the mission field. Joining with Christians from other traditions in a common witness, these pioneer evangelists formed ecumenical missionary societies. In many countries, these led to the establishment of indigenous churches that, to this day, enjoy historic ties to more than one European or North American denomination.

Presbyterians were instrumental in forming large-scale ecumenical organizations like the World Council of Churches and the World Communion of Reformed Churches. On a smaller scale, local councils of churches and ministerial associations can often be counted upon to have a Presbyterian representative chairing the meeting.

Ecumenism is imprinted on the Presbyterian denominational genome.

Inclusiveness and Representation

Related to the work of mutual forbearance is the principle of representation. This standard requires nominating committees and councils to make special efforts to ensure that elected groups—especially those charged with decision making—reflect not only the traditional Presbyterian parity between teaching and ruling elders, but also demographic distinctives such as gender, age, ethnicity, and disability. The theological groundwork for representation is laid out in F-1.0403, "Unity in Diversity":

> The unity of believers in Christ is reflected in the rich diversity of the Church's membership. In Christ, by the power of the Spirit, God unites persons through baptism regardless of race, ethnicity, age, sex, disability, geography, or theological conviction. There is therefore no place in the life of the Church for discrimination against any person. The Presbyterian Church (U.S.A.) shall guarantee full participation and representation in its worship, governance, and emerging life to all persons or groups within its membership. No member shall be denied participation or representation for any reason other than those stated in this *Constitution*.

> The only reason for denying a person membership in the Presbyterian

Church (U.S.A.), according to G-1.0302, is one "related to profession of faith."

This statement has particular significance and power in light of Martin Luther King Jr.'s oft-quoted observation that "Sunday morning at 11:00 a.m. is the most segregated hour in American life." Sadly, King's statement continues to ring true for a great many congregations. Presbyterian churches have often been at the forefront of civil-rights efforts, but many still find it difficult to attract a membership reflecting the full racial-ethnic diversity of their surrounding communities. Efforts to establish new racial-ethnic or multiethnic churches and to encourage existing congregations to become more diverse have yielded only limited success.

The church has had more success in increasing the representation of women in governance. The former Presbyterian Church, U.S.A. began ordaining women as deacons in 1922, as ruling elders in 1930, and as teaching elders in 1956. While it took some time after those early, historic ordinations for the church to ordain women in significant numbers, women now outnumber men on many sessions and boards of deacons. Progress was slower with fully welcoming women as teaching elders. It was not until the mid-1970s that large numbers of Presbyterian women began enrolling in seminary master of divinity programs. Close to half of MDiv enrollment in Presbyterian Church (U.S.A.) seminaries is now female, and in some schools more than half. With respect to pastoral positions, however, female teaching elders still report that they encounter a discouraging reality known as "the stained-glass ceiling": men continue to be called as pastors of larger congregations at a higher rate than women.

The section on "Participation and Representation" instructs all councils to "give full expression to the rich diversity of the church's membership . . . , [to] provide for full participation and access to representation in decisionmaking and employment practices," and to develop "procedures and mechanisms" for accomplishing this (G-3.0103). Councils higher than the session are given specific instructions to establish committees on representation to conduct periodic diversity audits. So important is the independence of such committees that they are given direct, high-level access to the council and are prohibited from being merged with any other committee.

Moderators

So important is this Historic Principle that the *Book of Order* arranges for each council to have its own mutual-forbearance officer. That person is the moderator. In session meetings, the moderator is nearly always the pastor; in fact, sessions are not permitted to meet at all unless the designated moderator or a duly appointed substitute is present (G-1.0504).

Only sessions have an ex-officio moderator. In presbytery and synod meetings and in the General Assembly, the moderator is an elected officer. These moderators are ruling or teaching elders who are chosen for their experience, wisdom, listening skills, decisiveness, knowledge of parliamentary procedure, and—most important of all—humility.

Moderators are given authority "for preserving order and for conducting efficiently the business of the body" (G-3.0104). While that may sound, at first glance, like an entirely obvious statement, in fact it gives moderators significant power. Well aware of the potential for power to be abused, Presbyterians curb it by strictly limiting higher-council moderator terms to one year.

The most effective moderators are not passive, simply waiting for members of the council to present motions. The type of moderator that councils most appreciate is a proactive leader who is always thinking one or two steps ahead and suggesting ways to get business accomplished efficiently, while preserving the right of members to have their say.

For example, moderators need not wait for a motion to "move the previous question" (to close debate and proceed to vote). If they sense debate is lagging or growing repetitious, they can ask for a motion to end debate, or can simply ask, "Are you ready to proceed to a vote?" If they sense the body is getting confused about a complicated item of business, they can rule that the motion be "divided" (considered in bite-sized sections). If they are certain, at five minutes past the docketed time for the lunch recess, the body is just about to conclude the present item of business, and someone rises to move "the order of the day" to enforce the prearranged recess time, they can simply decline to entertain the motion, reassuring the body that the morning's business is nearly completed and that immediately recessing will cost them more time in the long run.

Occasionally, moderators who lead proactively in this way may cause some members to fear they have overstepped their authority. Should such an objection be raised, a wise moderator will instantly suggest—in as calm and neutral a voice as possible—that anyone who feels uncomfortable with the ruling always has the ability to move to "appeal the chair" (to have the body vote on whether or not to sustain the ruling).

While it may at first seem like foolishness for moderators to invite a motion questioning their own authority, it is in fact a wise and self-assured response. It is as though the moderator is handing the gavel to the body, confident they will hand it right back. Such a response conveys a powerful message to the body: that they as a group are in charge (which, in fact, they are). It will cause them to feel relieved and empowered. New moderators need to do this sort of thing only a few times before the body concludes that their leader's highest priority is to make sure the business is being conducted fairly and expeditiously under the guidance of the Holy Spirit. The council that has come to that sort of conclusion will cheerfully hand its moderator all sorts of informal authority, and will apply peer pressure to resist future rebellions from the floor.

As long as a parliamentarian is present (often this is the clerk, although someone else may be specially appointed to that role), moderators do not have to have an encyclopedic knowledge of *Robert's Rules*. It is neither a sign of weakness nor incompetence to refer a point of order (a procedural question) to the parliamentarian for advice—although, in the end, it is the moderator, rather than the parliamentarian, who must issue the ruling. The body is not looking for their moderator to be the fount of all parliamentary wisdom. What the council most desires is to feel assured that someone fair minded and assertive, who has the group's best interests at heart, is in charge.

During their term of service, moderators do need to resist speaking for or against most motions, confining their remarks to procedural matters. That can be a hard discipline, at first, for those who are used to playing an active role in meetings, but it is essential. Should the body get the impression that their moderator is partisan, things will quickly begin to go badly. *Robert's Rules* does give moderators, as members of the body, the right to vote, but most moderators wisely decline to exercise that right (except, of course, for secret-ballot votes, or perhaps to break a tie).

In her helpful pamphlet *Parliamentary Procedures in the Presbyterian Church (U.S.A.)*—published by the Office of the General Assembly in 2000—Marianne L. Wolfe identifies three basic principles of parliamentary procedure. These explain not only the "how" of parliamentary rules, but also the "why." Moderators who internalize these foundational principles will quickly earn the respect of the members of the body.

First, *the rights and the unity of the body shall be preserved*. This is the reason certain motions are considered "privileged," taking precedence over other motions. Two examples of motions of personal privilege that can contribute to unity are to take a brief recess and to pause for prayer.

Certain procedural motions require a two-thirds supermajority vote. Generally, if *Robert's Rules* includes such a requirement, it is because such a motion could potentially threaten members' rights. The motion to "move the previous question" (end debate) is an example. Most people have seen this motion used coercively, as proponents of the main motion rush the measure toward a vote. *Robert's* wisely requires a two-thirds majority, so the body is assured that a large percentage of its members is indeed ready to move on. The same is true of a motion to "suspend the rules." The assumption here is that standing rules have been adopted to protect someone's rights, and such an action should therefore not be taken without a fair degree of unanimity.

Second, *the will of the majority shall prevail*. Wolfe points out that his principle is not about preserving rights, but about the mutual search for truth (not to mention getting business done expeditiously).

Majority rule is highly pragmatic. There is nothing magical nor mysterious about a majority's decision. Councils can—and do—sometimes err (as both the Westminster Confession, 6.175, and the *Book of Order*'s second Historical Principle, F-3.0102, affirm). Wolfe makes the insightful point that the goal of majority voting is not to certify the truth—as though parliamentary bodies were some kind of oracle—but rather to unite the entire group in a mutual search for truth. The moderator can model such an attitude by adopting a user-friendly tone, treating members with courtesy and patience when they ask how to accomplish a particular goal.

Third, *the rights of the minority shall be protected.* This is an especially important value for church meetings, as compared to other parliamentary settings. As the 1990 Brief Confession of Faith puts it, "The Spirit gives us courage . . . to hear the voices of people long silenced" (10.4). Wolfe cites John Knox, who once said of the lonely role of prophets that "[a] man with God is always in the majority."

From time to time, parliamentary procedure comes in for criticism in church circles. This may happen after a particularly contentious struggle that has included a good bit of dithering over procedural questions. It is easy to understand how veterans of several frustrating parliamentary experiences may begin to question whether there is not, in fact, a better way. Some people may begin talking about nonparliamentary, consensus-building sorts of decision-making processes.

At times, such procedures may be helpful, but they can also be manipulative in subtle ways. Sometimes those proposing alternative methods imply that it is somehow less than Christian to disagree. Consequently, the minority—not wanting to seem unchristian—suppresses their disagreement, leading to resentment that can simmer just beneath the surface of community life. Such suppressed anger may cause more damage to unity than if the minority viewpoint had been voiced in vigorous debate.

Wolfe also makes this hugely insightful comment: "The church protects its minority as if it were protecting its future." This observation is based on an oft-repeated occurrence in Presbyterian history. Whenever the church undergoes a sea change on some difficult, long-debated issue, the new majority position was itself a minority position for a great many years before. For this reason alone, the church is well advised to protect the rights of its minority. Not every minority position grows steadily in support until the church finally accepts it, but this happens often enough that the church is wise to be discerning and gracious as it deals with dissenters.

A final observation about parliamentary procedure: it is useful to picture the hierarchy of motions as though they were rungs on a ladder. As with any ladder, what goes up must come down. The ladder climber who touches a rung on the way up must eventually touch it again on the way down. Only one main motion is in order at any given time; to accept more than one would be like trying to climb two ladders at once. As any housepainter can attest, that is not a wise idea.

The main motion is the bottom rung of the ladder. Someone makes an amendment, which brings the body up to rung number two. Should an amendment to the amendment appear, that is a third rung. If someone then moves to commit (or refer) the whole matter to a committee for further study, that is a fourth rung.

Should the motion to commit subsequently fail, it is time to step back down to the third rung. The body continues the debate where they left off, considering the amendment to the amendment. Once that is settled, either yea or nay, the body stands on the second rung once again. Eventually, the group returns to the main motion—either amended or not, however the voting on the second rung turned out. It is important to step on each rung in order, so as not to skip any on the descent. As our friend the painter can attest, that is likewise not a good thing.

That sounds simple enough, but life in a council meeting gets even more interesting after one or more of the five privileged motions is factored in: to call for the order of the day, to raise a question of privilege, to take a recess, to adjourn, or the relatively rare "to fix a time at which to adjourn." These motions have no place on the ladder at all. They always take precedence over everything else, because they do not relate to any single item of business. They protect the rights, prerogatives, or comfort of the body at large. They are always in order, even if a main motion is already on the floor.

Robert's Rules is about more than just rules of order. The book also contains rules of decorum. These are not as familiar to most people, but they should be. The rules of decorum are all about extending grace and courtesy to one another. This ought to be perfectly obvious in a church meeting— although sometimes, in the heat of controversy, the basic obligations of civility may be forgotten for a time.

Two rules of decorum are particularly useful when it comes to the discipline of mutual forbearance. The first is to avoid referring to one another by name during debate. This helps keep the emotional heat from soaring up into triple digits. There is a world of difference, emotionally speaking, between saying, "John here is completely wrong in his discussion of this point," and saying, "My colleague from Old Westminster Church is completely wrong in his discussion of this point." The third-person form of address may sound stilted and old-fashioned, but it reflects long-established wisdom about how to treat fellow Christians kindly and with respect.

The second useful rule of decorum, in the service of mutual forbearance, is that of never directly addressing fellow members in debate, but speaking only to the moderator. Such triangulation may feel odd and unnatural at first, but there is good reason for it. Most people can recall watching a parliamentary debate that quickly grew uncomfortably heated and personal. Very likely, that happened because participants in the debate stopped looking toward the moderator. They turned, instead, to speak directly to one another—and as soon as they did, the temperature of the debate jumped ten degrees or so. Referring to one another in the third person and addressing remarks to the moderator are practical ways of enhancing civility.

To conclude our discussion of the Fifth Historic Principle, the best general advice for moderators as agents of mutual forbearance is firmly and benevolently to use the full extent of the power the *Book of Order* and *Robert's Rules* entrusts to them. Moderators are accorded that authority for a reason: to serve the members of the body by helping them to accomplish their work fairly, efficiently, and faithfully, to the glory of God.

Chapter 10

ELECTION BY THE PEOPLE

> That though the character, qualifications, and authority of Church officers are laid down in the Holy Scriptures, as well as the proper method of their investiture and institution, yet the election of the persons to the exercise of this authority, in any particular society, is in that society. (F-3.0106)

A leading cause of the American Revolution was the perception that authority was being imposed on the thirteen colonies from afar. For most of the activists who dumped tea into Boston harbor, it was not taxation as such that was the issue. It was the fact that the tea tax had been established by the far-off British Parliament, which included no members from the colonies. "No taxation without representation" became the battle cry.

It is no surprise, therefore, that when the commissioners to America's first Presbyterian General Assembly gathered in Philadelphia to approve their Form of Government—not so many years after events like the Boston Tea Party—they established the foundational principle that "the election of the persons to the exercise of this authority, in any particular society, is in that society."

Being Presbyterians, they resisted pure democracy along the lines of the New England town meeting. They knew, from tales their European Reformed ancestors had told of the excesses of the extreme fringe of the Anabaptist movement, how chaotic radical congregationalism could turn out to be. Steering a course between the Scylla of tyrannical episcopacy and the Charybdis of anarchic congregationalism, the members of that first General Assembly accepted the necessity that, in their new church, some members would inevitably have to govern others. As they made provision for these elected councils, they made sure they moved decision making as close to the grass roots as possible.

This principle has stood the Presbyterian Church in good stead ever since. At certain pressure points in church history, as conflict raged and schism loomed, the church has restored itself to equilibrium by raising the standard of the Sixth Historic Principle: strictly applying the dictum that "the election of the persons to the exercise of this authority, in any particular society, is in that society."

Debates over Ordination Standards

A curious consequence of the Presbyterian system of government is that, when simmering theological conflicts burst into open flame, the flash point is often a question of ordination standards. Because the proclamation of the Word is so essential to the Presbyterian ethos, the selection, education, and examination of teaching elders is of crucial importance. Examinations of candidates for ordination are among the few occasions when presbyters from across the theological spectrum engage in theological debate—as some candidates have learned to their dismay, hunkered down between the opposing battle lines as theological artillery shells whistle by overhead.

In 2011, the church applied this principle by removing constitutional language requiring those being examined for ordination to practice "fidelity within the covenant of marriage between a man and a woman or chastity in singleness." Out of consideration for their fellow presbyters' freedom of conscience, the General Assembly and the presbyteries moved the decision making closer to the grassroots level. It was a classic Presbyterian response, a middle way.

As such, it upset purists on both sides. Extreme conservatives preferred to see the old standard retained across the church. Extreme liberals preferred to see the new openness universally enforced, even in the most conservative presbyteries. As it happened, neither side got everything it wanted. The middle way prevailed.

A phrase cited with some frequency, prior to and during the presbyteries' voting on that amendment, was "the balkanization of the church." This expression refers to the map of the Balkan peninsula in southeastern Europe, a crazy quilt of overlapping nationalities and ethnicities. Some predicted that the change in ordination standards would result in a balkanized church, a loose confederation of presbyteries, each doing what it thinks right in its own eyes, enjoying little unity.

This has not proven to be the case. Ordaining presbyteries have the responsibility to examine new members—both ordinands and teaching elders transferring from another presbytery—in person. Their decision is both locally informed and is made on behalf of the whole church. It calls for mutual forbearance, trusting that the presbytery from which the new member is coming has exercised oversight faithfully and well. Even so, if something about the person being examined seems not quite right to the majority, they have every right to vote not to sustain the examination. That is not balkanization. It is simply Presbyterianism.

Another phrase that has come up frequently in debates over ordination standards is "ordination rights." This is a misnomer, because nowhere does the *Book of Order* speak of any such rights. There is no right to ordination in the Presbyterian Church. There is only the right of a society to elect its own members. Those who enter the preparation for ministry process can claim no right to be ordained at the conclusion of that process. They have only the right to present themselves for examination—after their presbytery has certified them ready, and after they have been provisionally offered a call to a presbytery-validated ministry. The calling presbytery does have the obligation to follow constitutional standards of representation in not categorically excluding anyone for the reasons prohibited in F-1.0403, but this places them under no obligation to decide one way or another in an individual case.

Electing Ruling Elders and Deacons

The Seventh Historic Principle is restated in G-2.0102, "Ordered Ministries": "The government of this church is representative, and the right of God's people to elect presbyters and deacons is inalienable. Therefore, no person can be placed in any ordered ministry in a congregation or council of the church except by election of that body."

This does not mean, however, that there are not procedures congregations must follow in electing ruling elders and deacons. Congregations must elect a nominating committee, "drawn from and representative of its membership" (G-2.0401). That committee must follow procedures that "shall express the rich diversity of the congregation's membership and shall guarantee participation and inclusiveness" with reference to the representation standards of F-1.0403. It must be composed of "at least three active members of the congregation, and shall include at least one ruling elder who is currently serving on the session." The requirement that the nominating committee include at least three members at large from the congregation is a safeguard against the session taking over the nomination process, making itself into a self-perpetuating group. In addition, "the pastor shall serve ex officio and without vote."

The involvement of pastors in the work of the nominating committee is important. Often, pastors are aware of pertinent information concerning the suitability of members to engage in ordered ministry, some of it confidential. Pastors should cultivate a strong relationship of trust with the nominating committee so that they may occasionally suggest that a given person may not be the strongest of choices, without having to provide specific details.

Christian stewardship practices are one of many factors relevant to the committee's decision. Pastors generally have access to individual financial giving records—information members of the nominating committee will likely not have.

The question of whether or not pastors ought to have access to individual giving records remains a matter of spirited discussion in some congregations. Generally, expecting the pastor to have no knowledge of member giving reflects a weak theology of stewardship that fails to see giving as a barometer of Christian spiritual commitment. Such information, of course, must always be understood from a proportionate-giving (percentage-of-income) perspective, not according to the total amounts individuals give. Simony—the purchasing of ecclesiastical offices with money—is one of the oldest sins in the church and can never be tolerated (see Acts 8:9–24). Nominations must never be offered as a quid pro quo in exchange for substantial gifts, as can be the case in some secular nonprofit organizations.

Pastors must refrain from trying to run the nominating committee, either directly or by proxy. Their role is to advise, not to direct. They may suggest names for consideration, but only to supplement the list of names committee members have already identified. Sometimes nominating committee chairs who are unsure of themselves may defer to the pastor, attempting to pass off their responsibilities. The pastor's most appropriate response is to deflect such attempts.

It is appropriate for pastors to train members of the nominating committee, orienting them to the constitutional requirements of their task. Committee members should strive to understand their work as a matter of discerning spiritual gifts rather than recruiting volunteers to fill slots on a roster. Service as a deacon or ruling elder is not a matter of volunteering. It is a matter of responding to God's call, communicated both through personal spiritual discernment and through the voice of the congregation.

Congregations have various traditions with respect to the particular form the nominating committee's report takes. The *Book of Order* provides no specific guidance on this question. In some congregations, the committee is expected to submit a slate of nominees that corresponds exactly to the number of vacancies. In others, the committee is encouraged to present more names than there are vacancies. The second option presents potential difficulties for those whose names are submitted but who are not subsequently selected. Having been encouraged prayerfully to consider the invitation from the committee as a potential call from God, then to discover that the committee has said the very same thing to more people than can be elected, may be a disillusioning experience.

The one requirement the *Book of Order* does make with respect to the slate of nominees is that opportunity must be given, in the congregational meeting, for nominations to be made from the floor (G-2.0401). In most congregations, floor nominations are uncommon. If such nominations are a frequent occurrence, that may be a warning sign of conflict or factionalism. Should it happen that there are more nominees than there are vacant positions—either by reason of floor nominations or because the committee has presented a slate with a surplus of names—it is advisable to conduct the vote by secret ballot. Clerks of session should always prepare for this eventuality, having paper available for ballots in case they are needed.

It is generally unwise for the nominating committee to come to the congregational meeting with an incomplete slate, expecting the remaining vacancies to be filled by floor nominations. The few seconds available for a member who has been nominated to decide whether or not to accept are not adequate for proper discernment, nor can the nominating committee discreetly ponder any suggestions of names that may be inappropriate.

The *Book of Order* speaks of "Preparation for Ministry as a Ruling Elder or Deacon" (G-2.0402). The similarity to the language used for teaching elders is deliberate. Service as a ruling elder or deacon *is* ministry. While the preparation for ordination to these orders of ministry is not described in nearly so much detail as for teaching elders, it is equally important:

> The session shall provide a period of study and preparation, after which the session shall examine them as to their personal faith; knowledge of the doctrine, government, and discipline contained in the Constitution of the church; and the duties of the ministry. The session shall also confer with them as to their willingness to undertake the ministry appropriate to the order. (G-2.0402)

The plan for the "period of study and preparation" is up to the session to determine. It is common for the pastor to take on this responsibility at the session's request. The *Book of Order* and the *Book of Confessions* should be primary texts.

The Session's examination of the newly elected officers is highly important—if for no other reason than to provide a final screening, in the event that a person who is inappropriate for service has been nominated from the floor and elected. The examination may be accomplished in a variety of ways. It probably will not take the form of session members sitting on a panel, firing theological and polity questions at those who have been elected. Dividing the session into small groups for examination in a more conversational format is more congenial and may accomplish the goal just as effectively.

Congregational Meetings

Ruling elders and deacons are elected at a meeting of the congregation. Apart from business related to the calling of a pastor or dissolving the pastoral relationship, electing such leaders is one of the very few specific powers belonging to congregations. In G-1.0503, the *Book of Order* limits the items of business that may be considered at congregational meetings to the following:

- electing ruling elders, deacons, or trustees (if the congregation has a separate board of trustees)
- calling pastors

- changing existing pastoral relationships, revising the terms of call or considering a request to dissolve a pastoral call
- buying, mortgaging, or selling real estate
- requesting the presbytery to grant an exemption to the usual requirements for term length and / or term rotation for ruling elders and deacons (G-2.0404)
- approving, changing, or dissolving a plan for a joint congregational witness

Congregations are required to meet at least annually (G-1.0501). At the annual general meeting, any of the above-mentioned items of business is in order. If a special meeting is called, the items of business to be considered must be listed in the call to the meeting. Nothing other than those items listed in the call may be considered.

Congregational meetings may be called in one of three ways:

- by the session
- by the presbytery
- by the session, when requested in writing by one-fourth of the active members (G-1.0502)

The session will call the vast majority of congregational meetings. The other two options are useful in times of controversy. The presbytery may call a congregation together for any purpose, but that is only likely to happen if the presbytery is concerned about either the pastor's or the session's leadership, or both. There is also a provision for members of the congregation to call a meeting through a petition process. Should church members succeed in collecting petition signatures from one-fourth of the active members, the session has no other option but to call the meeting (G-1.0502).

Calling a Pastor

Apart from electing ruling elders and deacons, the most important responsibility congregations have is calling a pastor (or associate pastor, or co-pastor). We have already seen how, in classic Reformed thinking, the acclamation of the people is an essential feature of the outer call to ministry. The call process is how it takes place.

At the heart of a congregation's call process is their election of a pastor nominating committee (G-2.0802). Representatives of the presbytery will begin consulting with the session about the election of such a committee as soon as it becomes apparent there is going to be a pastoral vacancy. The presbytery will likely have its own specific guidelines for church leaders to follow in searching for a pastor, above and beyond the details specified in the *Book of Order*. In order to encourage an open search, presbyteries commonly insist that pastor nominating committees not be elected until the former pastor has departed.

The *Book of Order* stipulates that this committee must be "representative of the whole congregation." In addition to the usual demographic factors described under the heading of "representation," the phrase "whole congregation" means that the pastor nominating committee cannot be composed exclusively of session members. In order to ensure that it truly operates as a congregational committee, the presbytery will likely require that a majority of its members come from the congregation at large.

The following paragraph describing the call process is not very detailed, because presbyteries are expected to adopt their own specific policies and regulations for pastor nominating committees to follow: "According to the process of the presbytery and prior to making its report to the congregation, the pastor nominating committee shall receive and consider the presbytery's counsel on the merits, suitability, and availability of those considered for the call. When the way is clear for the committee to report to the congregation, the committee shall notify the session, which shall call a congregational meeting" (G-2.0803).

Typically, the presbytery—through its committee on ministry or similar group—assigns a liaison to consult with the pastor nominating committee at most or all of its meetings. That person guides the committee as it conducts a "mission study"—a detailed self-assessment of the congregation's composition, community setting, and mission priorities. The results of this study inform the writing of a Church Information Form, or CIF. The CIF must be approved by both the session and the presbytery, typically through its committee on ministry or similar group, before it can be filed with the Presbyterian Church (U.S.A.)'s online Church Leadership Connection. Teaching elders and approved candidates for ministry may review the information on that Web site.

The pastor nominating committee may specify certain parameters describing the types of individuals they are willing to consider, such as the geographic region from which they come and their level of experience. Whether they limit their search by introducing such restrictions or whether they keep it wide open, the committee is required to comply with the usual requirements of inclusion and representation.

Under the guidance of their presbytery advisor, the pastor nominating committee narrows the field of individuals who have submitted Ministry Information Forms (or MIFs). They may review recordings or videos of their leading candidates' sermons. They may conduct preliminary interviews by telephone or by Internet conferencing before arriving at a short list of people they will interview face to face. Typically, they will hear these individuals preach in person, either by traveling to another church where the person is already preaching or—if the person lives far away—by asking the presbytery to set up a "neutral pulpit" guest-preaching arrangement in a nearby church. Candidates never preach, at this stage, to the congregation for which they are applying, because that could violate the confidentiality that surrounds the search process. The pastor nominating committee needs to complete its work in private, without being lobbied by members of the congregation.

When the committee has reached a decision, there are several things that need to happen. These may take place in the order described below, or they may happen in a slightly different order, according to presbytery policy:

- Advising the candidate that the person is the committee's choice and giving the person an opportunity provisionally to accept the offer
- Negotiating the "terms of call"—the financial compensation and benefits (G-2.0804)
- A presbytery reference check, whereby an official of the presbytery (typically the executive presbyter, if there is one) contacts his or her counterpart in the candidate's presbytery to make sure there are no problems or outstanding issues that could present difficulties in the new position
- Approval by the committee on ministry or similar group, indicating their judgment that the candidate is a good match for the congregation
- Notifying the session of whom the committee has chosen, after which the session calls a congregational meeting
- Along with the call to the congregational meeting, the committee's communicating to the congregation biographical details about the candidate
- The candidate's preaching in a regular worship service of the congregation, after which a congregational meeting is held, at which the congregation decides whether or not to extend the call through the presbytery and—if the decision is affirmative—approves the terms of call
- The candidate's examination by the presbytery (or, according to its rules, by a designated committee or administrative commission), at which time both the terms of call and the plans for the installation service are approved
- The presbytery's extending the call to the candidate, who formally accepts it
- If he or she is presently serving a congregation, the candidate's notifying that congregation and presbytery of his or her acceptance of the new call

- Formalizing the transfer of membership by the stated clerks of the two presbyteries
- A service of installation (which may include ordination as well, if the pastor-elect is a candidate under care) conducted by the presbytery (Services of ordination and/or installation are services of the presbytery, even though they typically take place in the congregation's place of worship [G-2.0805].)

Dissolving a Pastoral Relationship

The flip side of calling a pastor is the dissolution of a pastoral relationship. This may happen for a variety of reasons—some in generally happy circumstances (although with understandable sadness at the parting), others in more problematic situations.

The basic process is described as follows:

An installed pastoral relationship may be dissolved only by the presbytery. Whether the teaching elder, the congregation, or the presbytery initiates proceedings for dissolution of the relationship, there shall always be a meeting of the congregation to consider the matter and to consent, or decline to consent, to dissolution. (G-2.0901)

There are several ways the dissolution of a pastoral relationship may be initiated.

- *At the pastor's request* (G-2.0902). If the circumstances are generally happy, this is fairly straightforward. The pastor makes the request of the presbytery, also notifying the session. The session calls a congregational meeting, at which the congregation votes either to concur or not to concur with the dissolution. If the request is not to concur (which is rare), the presbytery will want to investigate.
- *At the congregation's request* (G-2.0903). The session calls a congregational meeting for that purpose and requests the presbytery to appoint a moderator for the meeting. If the pastor agrees, the congregation votes to request dissolution. If the pastor does not agree, the pastor is given an opportunity to state the reasons why this should not be done. If the pastor fails to appear, or if the pastor's reasons are deemed insufficient, the congregation votes to request dissolution. In the rare event that the pastor's reasons against dissolution are deemed sufficient, the presbytery would undoubtedly initiate some kind of mediation or conflict-resolution process. In any event, the presbytery often insists that the

congregation continue salary and benefits for a period of time, allowing the pastor to have transitional support while seeking a new call.

– *By action of the presbytery.* This option is described as follows: "The presbytery may inquire into reported difficulties in a congregation and may dissolve the pastoral relationship if, after consultation with the teaching elder, the session, and the congregation, it finds the church's mission under the Word imperatively demands it" (G-2.0904).

The phrase, "the church's mission under the Word imperatively demands it" indicates one of the presbytery's most significant powers under the *Book of Order*. The judgment as to whether or not the church's mission does imperatively demand the dissolution of a pastoral relationship covers a variety of circumstances and is entirely up to the presbytery to decide. The presbytery is required only to *consult* with the pastor, session, and congregation. None of them is required to concur in order for the presbytery's decision to be implemented.

This is an extreme option, but sometimes circumstances do warrant it. Generally the presbytery will try to use persuasion and negotiation to convince one or more of the parties to concur with that judgment. If it is not possible, and the presbytery is convinced that great harm will come from leaving the pastoral relationship intact, the presbytery can remove the pastor on its own authority.

Ethics Related to Former Pastoral Relationships

Even if the circumstances of the dissolution of a pastoral relationship are generally happy, problems can arise afterward if the former pastor is not scrupulous about following certain protocols with respect to communicating with former parishioners. The personal and emotional dynamics connected with pastoral ministry are such that it takes time for members of the congregation to form a bond with their new pastor. During the period when this is happening—which can take several years, and sometimes longer in the case of certain members who enjoyed a particularly close relationship with the former pastor—the new ministry is vulnerable to significant damage as a result of things the former pastor may decide to do.

The most serious damage is caused by the former pastor providing certain pastoral services connected with life transitions: baptisms, weddings, and funerals, as well as pastoral-care contacts such as hospital visits and counseling. There will always be some members who feel a stronger attachment to the former pastor than to the present one. When they or members of their families need such pastoral services, their first inclination may be to contact the former pastor and ask him or her to provide them, even if they have been informed this is not advisable. Some former pastors have a hard time saying no when asked to help former parishioners in need; so the *Book of Order* provides this firm guidance: "After the dissolution of the pastoral relationship, former pastors and associate pastors shall not provide their pastoral services to members of their former congregations without the invitation of the moderator of session" (G-2.0905).

There is more that needs to be said, beyond this. If former pastors follow the minimal direction the *Book of Order* provides, they are still putting their successor in an awkward spot. The problem is that, if a former pastor receives such a request from a church member and responds by explaining that he or she would like to help but cannot do so without the approval of the new pastor, that puts the new pastor in an impossible situation. If either the church member or the former pastor subsequently contacts the new pastor, it is difficult for the new pastor to say no without appearing jealous and insecure—despite the fact that the *Book of Order* backs the new pastor 100 percent in declining to issue the invitation. The trick is for both pastors to work out a prearranged agreement to respond in such a way as to strengthen the new ministry.

Here is an example of an agreement between the new and the former pastor that makes both of them look good. The former pastor says to the new pastor: "I pledge to keep you fully informed of all requests for pastoral services I receive from members of your church. I would prefer to decline most of these offers, but—if it is agreeable to you—I would like to accept a very small number of them. In every case, when I receive such a request, I will say no, explaining that it is now your responsibility, as pastor, to provide pastoral services to members.

"If this is a request I would like to accept, I will telephone you immediately and inform you of the request. If it is an invitation I am not interested in accepting, I will tell you so, and you can reach out to the family. If, on the other hand, it is an invitation I would like to accept, I will inform you that I would be interested in co-officiating.

"The decision to issue such an invitation to me is entirely up to you. If you decline to issue the invitation, that ends the matter. If you do issue the invitation, you can then reach out to the family and tell them you have asked me to assist you in conducting the service. This keeps the family happy, makes both of us look good and—because of your role as primary officiant—reinforces the fact that this is your job now."

Categories of Teaching Elders

Presbyteries have responsibility to sort their teaching-elder members into one of three categories. It is easiest to explain these categories by discussing them in reverse order.

The first category is *honorably retired* (G-2.0503c). Retired members of presbytery continue to have the privilege of the floor in presbytery meetings, although their attendance at such meetings is optional. A record is kept of retired members' attendance, but there are no negative ramifications for their continued presbytery membership if they do not attend. They are permitted to keep their membership in the presbytery from which they retired, or they may ask to be transferred to another presbytery closer to their new home. Honorably retired members who are in good health form a significant pool of talent and experience. Many continue to serve their presbyteries faithfully and well, as they are able.

The second membership category is *at-large* (G-2.0503b). These teaching elders too have the privilege of the floor at presbytery meetings. Their attendance is required on the same basis as those in active service.

Teaching elders who are not retired may find themselves in this category for a variety of reasons. An interim pastor, or a pastor who has followed a spouse to a new place of employment, may have left a former position but has yet to find a new one. A parent may be caring for young children at home, or an adult child for an aging parent. Health problems may have led to temporary disability. The demands of advanced academic studies may make continued professional employment impractical for a time. Whatever the reason, presbyteries use the at-large category compassionately to care for the needs of their members in transitional

---

The decision as to whether or not to accept an honorably retired teaching elder by transfer from another presbytery is entirely up to the new presbytery. A few presbyteries located near popular retirement areas, seeking to balance the average age of their membership, have adopted policies restricting the number of retired teaching elders they will receive into membership. While such policies do accomplish their intended demographic effect, they also cause the presbytery to appear inhospitable—and to discard, sight unseen, substantial talents from which the presbytery's committees could benefit. Blanket exclusionary policies of this sort likely conflict with *Book of Order* guidelines for inclusion and representation because they discriminate on the basis of age.

times, giving them opportunities to continue to share their talents as they serve on committees of the presbytery. At-large status must be renewed annually.

As with honorably retired teaching elders, some presbyteries have adopted blanket policies of not receiving at-large members by transfer from other presbyteries, even if the teaching elder has relocated into the area of the new presbytery permanently, for family or other reasons. Again, such discriminatory policies are likely to be seen as inhospitable and shortsighted, for the same reasons as with the honorably retired.

The third, and typically largest, membership category is teaching elders in *validated ministries* (G-2.0503a). Ideally, all members of the presbytery who are neither honorably retired nor at-large will be in this category.

Each year, the presbytery is required to vote to validate the ministries of its teaching elders who are not honorably retired. The validation decision applies not to the teaching elder personally, but to the teaching elder's *work*—although persistence in an unvalidated ministry, over the objections of the presbytery, could lead to disciplinary action that has negative ramifications for the teaching elder's ordination.

A committee of the presbytery—most often the committee on ministry—is in charge of the data gathering for this task. The positions of those serving congregations of the presbytery (or of a partner denomination) in any sort of pastoral role, as well as those who work for another presbytery, a synod, the General Assembly, or any of its agencies, are automatically validated. For all others, the following criteria from G-2.0503a apply. A validated ministry must

1. demonstrate conformity with the mission of God's people in the world as set forth in Holy Scripture, The *Book of Confessions*, and the *Book of Order* of this church;
2. serve and aid others, and enable the ministry of others;
3. give evidence of theologically informed fidelity to God's Word;
4. be carried on in accountability for its character and conduct to the presbytery in addition to any organizations, agencies, and institutions served; and
5. include responsible participation in the deliberations, worship, and work of the presbytery and in the life of a congregation of this church or a church in correspondence with the PC(USA). (G-5.0201)

The first three criteria have to do with the nature of the work itself. For most presbyteries, specialized ministries such as hospital, hospice, military, or higher-education chaplaincy, or providing licensed pastoral counseling through a recognized agency are easily approved, as long as such teaching elders can submit evidence of their continued employment. Other positions may be validated as well, although the presbytery committee may have to dig a little for the information it needs to determine that the work does comply with the first three criteria.

The remaining two criteria have to do with the teaching elder's involvement in the presbytery. The presbytery should have sufficient engagement with the employing organization to certify supervisory accountability. The last criterion—responsible participation in the life both of the presbytery and of a congregation—is easily overlooked by some but is vitally important. Teaching elders in specialized ministry may indeed have "day jobs" that keep them busy, but they need to make time to be active in the presbytery as well. On Sunday mornings, or at other times when God's people gather, they need to be in worship as well—if not helping to lead worship by invitation of the pastor, then by joining in prayer and praise alongside members of the congregation.

It is easy for teaching elders in specialized ministries to get caught up in the many demands placed on them in their workplace. In particular, the performance evaluations and accountability structures belonging to that setting may naturally appear, to them, larger in importance than their presbytery's annual validation process. Even so, the presbytery relationship must not be neglected.

The final line of G-2.0502 provides a fitting benediction for all who serve Christ in settings other than congregations or councils of the church: "Teaching elders have membership in the presbytery by action of the presbytery itself, and no pastoral relationship may be established, changed, or dissolved without the approval of the presbytery." Membership in presbytery is not a lifetime right bestowed automatically along with ordination. It is an active relationship that, in order to remain healthy, must be nurtured and maintained.

Preparation for Ministry (Teaching Elders)

At the heart of the preparation for ministry process is a covenant relationship between presbyteries and those preparing to become teaching elders. It is divided into two phases: inquiry and candidacy (G-2.0601). Sometimes an earlier phase is discussed as well: that of "seeker." This term—which has no constitutional status—refers to those who have identified themselves as interested in ordained ministry but who have not yet been enrolled by their presbyteries as inquirers.

Former editions of the *Book of Order* spelled out a churchwide preparation for ministry process in great detail. In the interests of simplicity and flexibility, much of that detail has been removed from the present book. Those requirements did not disappear altogether. Most of them have ended up in an advisory handbook on the preparation-for-ministry process published by the General Assembly's Office on Preparation for Ministry. Although presbyteries are not as thoroughly bound by those requirements as they once were, nearly all of them voluntarily follow those guidelines.

Before becoming eligible for ordination, inquirers/candidates must first be members of a Presbyterian congregation for at least six months. After that, they must be in a formal relationship with the presbytery, through its committee on preparation for ministry (or another committee exercising those responsibilities) for at least two years (G-2.0602). This means the *minimum* time a person must be in the process is two and a half years. The event that sets that clock ticking is the date on which the presbytery votes to enroll the person as an inquirer. Considering the fact that there can be some waiting time before a space opens up on a busy committee's meeting agenda and the further fact that the typical MDiv degree can be completed in just under three years, it is imperative that enrollment as an inquirer take place as early as possible.

The process is designed so people can be enrolled as inquirers with a minimum of delay. Enrollment as an inquirer implies no endorsement by the presbytery. Presbyteries are meant to take this action on the strength of the session's recommendation that the person displays promise, without requiring much further information—other than, perhaps, an informational intake interview conducted by their committee. Presbyteries who introduce other requirements to be completed before the inquiry phase begins are doing their candidates a disservice, because such a practice can delay eligibility for ordination past the date of the candidate's seminary graduation.

The transition from inquirer to candidate is an important milestone, because it represents a qualified endorsement by the presbytery. There is still no guarantee of successful completion, but it means the presbytery has come to know the inquirer well enough to be generally optimistic about the outcome.

The prevailing feature of the candidacy process is *oversight* (G-2.0605). Comprehensive oversight may be something of a new experience for candidates, whose college and seminary degree programs exercised oversight mainly through discrete academic courses. Except for some occasional help from a faculty member serving as academic advisor—whose primary purpose is to help them choose the right classes in order to graduate on time—students are used to being left more or less on their own to pursue their individual interests. Based on their undergraduate experience, students naturally assume the academic degree is the ultimate prize at the end of the race, the credential they need in order to be ordained.

Based on past experience, this is a reasonable assumption. But it is mistaken. The seminary diploma is not the ultimate prize for which they are striving. Ordination is that prize; and the seminary faculty does not have the power to give it to them. Only the calling presbytery, where new graduates find their first position in ministry, has that power. The calling presbytery, in turn, depends heavily on the endorsement of the presbytery of care—the presbytery where the candidate's home church is located—before granting approval. That presbytery endorsement is far more valuable to the ministerial student, in the long run, than the seminary diploma.

Some students are slow to grasp that reality. They may grow frustrated with the requirements of their presbytery committee, seeing annual consultations as a distraction from their primary work in lecture hall and library. Some pay scant attention to additional course requirements the presbytery may impose, mistakenly assuming the graduation requirements in the seminary catalog are their only real concern. Some put more energy into preparing for final examinations for seminary courses than they do preparing for the standard ordination examinations—unaware that a passing grade on the ordination examinations is of infinitely greater interest to the committee on preparation for ministry than the difference between a B and an A in a seminary course.

Some too fail to anticipate the questions the committee on preparation for ministry will ask them during annual consultations. No one on the seminary faculty is likely to ask probing questions about their prayer life, how they manage stress, or what makes them feel certain God is calling them to ministry. The question of where—or whether—students attend Sunday worship is a matter of indifference to many seminary professors, but it will be high on the list of things their committee will ask about. From the standpoint of academic life, such questions may appear overly personal, even intrusive—but they have everything to do with predicting long-term success in ministry.

Some students fail to understand that they need proactively to manage their relationship with their presbytery committee. There are deadlines to remember, essays to write, psychological assessments to undergo—all according to a certain timetable, tied not to the seminary's academic calendar but to the tightly packed meeting schedule of the committee. Over the course of a three-year seminary degree, as many as one-third to one-half of the members of the committee may change, including the committee chair and the committee member serving as the candidate's liaison.

There are presbytery requirements related to field education work that may or may not coincide exactly with the seminary's graduation requirements. That fascinating field education assignment in nontraditional ministry may not prove so fascinating to the committee, who may be most concerned with seeing the candidate excel in a congregational setting—preferably a Presbyterian congregation (G-2.0606).

Seminaries manage the problem of faculty turnover by means of an academic transcript recording courses completed and grades earned. The presbytery has a transcript of sorts as well. It is the student's candidacy file. That file includes not only the most recent seminary transcript, but also reports of each consultation the student has had with the committee, recommendations, correspondence, psychological assessments, field-education supervisory reports, and certificates of completion of additional programs such as clinical pastoral education. It is essential that candidates keep a duplicate paper trail of evaluations, correspondence, and certificates of achievement, paying particular attention to documenting alternative routes the committee has approved to fulfilling constitutional requirements.

The following line from the *Book of Order* may cause tremendous difficulty if the student fails to notice it: "A candidate may not enter into negotiation for his or her service as a teaching elder without approval of the presbytery." The seminary graduation date may be looming, and the interview the seminary placement office has arranged with a pastor nominating committee may seem enticing, but if the presbytery committee has not yet granted permission to pursue a call—the precise language is "certified ready for examination for ordination, pending a call"—then entering into negotiations with a pastor nominating committee can cause a major rift between the candidate and the presbytery's committee (G-2.0607).

Ordinarily the committee must satisfy itself that students have fulfilled all of the following conditions before certifying them ready to negotiate for a call:

> a. a candidate's wisdom and maturity of faith, leadership skills, compassionate spirit, honest repute, and sound judgment;
> b. a transcript showing graduation, with satisfactory grades, at a regionally accredited college or university;
> c. a transcript from a theological institution accredited by the Association of Theological Schools acceptable to the presbytery, showing a course of study including Hebrew and Greek, exegesis of the Old and New Testaments using Hebrew and Greek, satisfactory grades in all areas of study, and graduation or proximity to graduation; and

d. satisfactory grades, together with the examination papers in the areas covered by any standard ordination examination approved by the General Assembly. (G-2.0607)

Students will likely notice that the *Book of Order* has a clause allowing most preparation for ministry requirements—other than passing grades on the standard ordination examinations—to be replaced with alternative procedures under certain circumstances (G-2.0610). They should never assume, however, that permission for such alternatives—which require a three-quarters majority vote of the entire presbytery—will be granted routinely.

With respect to ordination—when that time finally comes—it is ordinarily the presbytery of call that examines the candidate and conducts the ordination service rather than the presbytery of care (G-2.0702). Arrangements may be made for the presbytery of care to conduct the ordination service on behalf of the calling presbytery, but only if the calling presbytery grants permission.

The ordination service is a service of the presbytery, not the local congregation in which the service takes place. This means that, in submitting names of potential members of the ordination commission, candidates must consult closely with the ordaining presbytery, which has certain diversity, parity, and other requirements it must fulfill with respect to the membership of the commission. It is also well to remember that the moderator of the presbytery (or the moderator's designee) presides at the service. So it is a breach of protocol for the ordinand to specify which role the moderator will play. It is best to start by asking the moderator what he or she expects to do and only then—with the moderator's permission—begin assigning particular roles to others.

Chapter 11

CHURCH POWER

That all Church power, whether exercised by the body in general or in the way of representation by delegated authority, is only ministerial and declarative; that is to say, that the Holy Scriptures are the only rule of faith and manners; that no Church judicatory ought to pretend to make laws to bind the conscience in virtue of their own authority; and that all their decisions should be founded upon the revealed will of God. Now though it will easily be admitted that all synods and councils may err, through the frailty inseparable from humanity, yet there is much greater danger from the usurped claim of making laws than from the right of judging upon laws already made, and common to all who profess the gospel, although this right, as necessity requires in the present state, be lodged with fallible men. (F-3.0107)

In the waning days of the Second World War, British Prime Minister Winston Churchill and his Soviet counterpart, Premier Josef Stalin, were meeting together to discuss, among other things, the future of Poland. Churchill was warning Stalin that any heavy-handed actions on his part could complicate the Soviet Union's diplomatic relationship with the Vatican.

"How many divisions does the pope have?" Stalin retorted.

The dictator's remark was passed on in due course to Pope Pius XII. He issued his own curt response to Stalin: "You can tell my son Josef he will meet my divisions in heaven."

The exchange among these world leaders captures the exquisite irony of speaking about ecclesiastical power. The authors of the Historic Principles were well aware of this reality. This is why the Seventh Historic Principle realistically describes church power as "only ministerial and declarative."

Those two words seem, at first hearing, to make little sense in this context. The key is found in the historic meaning of "ministerial." We have already observed how "minister" means "servant." The founders are saying the church's power arises out of its weakness. Power deriving from servanthood is a paradoxical concept if ever there was one.

The church's power is also declarative. That means it flows from declarations, or words. A declarative sentence is one that imparts information

115

or reveals feelings. An imperative sentence compels action. It derives from the Latin *imperium*, which evokes the power of the Roman emperor. The church's speech is of the declarative rather than the imperative sort.

The only power the church has arises from the example of its servant-hood and the persuasive power of its words. In other words, the church's only authority is its moral authority.

This recalls the account, in Mark 1:21–28, of the people's response to Jesus' teaching in the synagogue at Capernaum: "They were astounded at his teaching, for he taught them as one having authority, and not as the scribes." Scribes in first-century Judaism were part of the power structure of the temple hierarchy. Their power derived from their office and from their training in expert legal interpretation. Jesus holds no such office. His disciples do address him as "rabbi," or teacher, but that is a largely honor-ific title. Nowhere in the Scriptures do we see Jesus claiming earthly power or authority for himself. On the contrary, in the story of his temptation in the wilderness, he spurns the devil's attempt to convince him to seize personal power. The quixotic nature of his travels across the countryside, trailed by his little band of followers, living off the land and depending on the generosity of people he meets, is a sort of antipower.

But Jesus' ministerial and declarative power—his radical servanthood and authoritative teaching, causing his followers' hearts to "burn within them" (Luke 24:32)—are without equal. As he engages in philosophi-cal discourse with Pontius Pilate, who embodies the awful power of the emperor, it is clear who wields true power. The procurator can shackle Jesus' wrists and ankles, but he cannot touch Jesus' spirit. Pilate has lost the moral high ground.

Civil and Ecclesiastical Power

The authors of the Historic Principles were well aware that they were founding a church under very different circumstances than their European counterparts. The wars of the Reformation had been fought in part because of the unquestioned assumption that the church must be *established*.

"Establishment" in the ecclesiastical sense means the church is inte-grally related to the state. The Church of Scotland, to this day, is a national church. Every time Queen Elizabeth II—titular head of the Church of Eng-land—crosses the border into Scotland, she becomes a Presbyterian. This strange circumstance is the consequence of the uniting of the crowns of England and Scotland under her ancestor, James I and VI. That makes the queen head of both national churches. The room in Edinburgh where the kirk's General Assembly meets is dominated by an imposing, thronelike chair reserved for the queen. Although the queen rarely attends—send-ing some member of the House of Lords to sit there, sleepily, through the debate—she retains the privilege of doing so. Her role as head of a

Presbyterian church is purely symbolic these days, but it recalls an earlier theocratic era.

We have seen how, in the religious wars of the sixteenth and seventeenth centuries, the outcome could only be winner-take-all. If Protestant rebels could convince the ruling authorities—by persuasion or force of arms—that their interpretation of Scripture was correct, they would win the prize of endorsement by the civil authorities, becoming the established national church. If they failed, they would be relegated to second-class, "nonconformist" status.

Although Calvin's official position in Geneva was ostensibly ecclesiastical, his moral authority over the Genevan Council was such that he effectively ruled over both church and state. The city government in his day was a theocracy.

The Heidelberg Catechism demonstrates such an understanding when it states that, in correcting wrongdoers, "the Christian church is dutybound to exclude such people, by the official use of the keys of the kingdom, until they reform their lives" (4.082). The Catechism names two keys, preaching and ecclesiastical discipline, that "open the kingdom of heaven to believers and close it to unbelievers" (4.083).

Years before the United Kingdom's Act of Toleration had been passed, the Westminster Confession demonstrated a growing understanding of appropriate boundaries between church and state. The 1647 edition of the document asserts:

> The Civil Magistrate may not assume to himself the administration of the Word and Sacraments, or the power of the Keyes of the Kingdome of Heaven: yet, he hath Authoritie, and it is his duetie, to take order, that Unitie and Peace be preserved in the Church, that the Truth of God be kept pure, and intire, that all Blasphemies and Heresies be suppressed, all corruptions and abuses in Worship and Discipline prevented, or reformed; and all the Ordinances of God duely settled, administered, and observed. For the better effecting whereof, he hath power to call Synods, to be present at them, and to provide that whatsoever is transacted in them, be according to the minde of God. (6.129, footnote)

When Reformed refugees made their way to Massachusetts in the early seventeenth century, they established theocratic governments in Plymouth and in the Massachusetts Bay colony. Although those colonies nominally

The Westminster Confession gives secular rulers the power to "call Synods," as the Emperor Constantine had done for the Council of Nicaea—and, indeed, as King James I had done for the Westminster Assembly itself (6.129, footnote).

owed allegiance to the British crown, in their day-to-day life they were governed by local church authorities.

We have seen how, when Parliament passed the Act of Toleration in 1689, during the reign of William and Mary, things began to change. For the first time, certain churches formerly branded nonconformist—including the Reformed church in England, now known as the United Reformed Church—were permitted to enter the mainstream. There was still an established church in England, but for the first time several other churches enjoyed a sanctioned, legal existence.

The Act of Toleration set a snowball of ecclesiastical change rolling slowly down a hill, gaining in size and speed. It continued to accelerate until it arrived, full grown, at the start of the American republic. The founders of the Presbyterian Church in the new nation knew the world had changed, and with it the church. They made the realistic assessment that, in a pluralistic democracy, church power can only be ministerial and declarative, and they designed their church accordingly. They took the extraordinary step of amending the Westminster Confession, removing the language recognizing secular rulers as official protectors of the church, by which they formerly had authority to convene church councils.

One of the earliest American ecclesiastical statements of the separation of church and state, this 1788 amendment—still a part of the *Book of Confessions*—declares:

> Civil magistrates may not . . . interfere in matters of faith. Yet, as nursing fathers, it is the duty of civil magistrates to protect the church of our common Lord, without giving the preference to any denomination of Christians above the rest. . . . And, as Jesus Christ hath appointed a regular government and discipline in his church, no law of any commonwealth should interfere with, let, or hinder, the due exercise thereof, among the voluntary members of any denomination of Christians, according to their own profession and belief. (6.129)

This is also one of the earliest occurrences anywhere of the word "denomination," referring to a church independent of the state.

Stated clerks and others who are experienced with professional-misconduct trials under the Rules of Discipline sometimes bump up against the boundary between church and state. Over many months, an investigating committee may have been conducting interviews and gathering evidence, eventually filing charges against a teaching elder (D-10.0201). All the while, the accused is meant to be planning a defense—selecting counsel, gathering evidence, and submitting the names of witnesses to the Permanent Judicial Commission. Abruptly, on the eve of the trial, the accused submits a terse letter to the stated clerk, as permitted in G-2.0407: "I renounce the jurisdiction of the Presbyterian Church (U.S.A.)."

The trial is off. It will never take place, because the teaching elder has quit not only his or her position as pastor, but the entire denomination. The alleged victims may yearn for their day in court, but they will never get it. The accused is now beyond the reach of the church—although, depending on the offense, there may be further recourse in the secular criminal or civil courts.

The church's ministerial and declarative power has an impact on the situation as long as the accused remains subject to its moral authority. Renunciation of jurisdiction, however, has removed that person from any setting in which that power may be felt. Like the laughing speeder looking back at the sheriff across the county line, in stepping away from the church the accused has also stepped beyond the range of ecclesiastical power.

The Power of Individuals

There is one place in the *Book of Confessions* that refers to church power as exercised by individuals. The section from the Second Helvetic Confession entitled "The Power of Ministers of the Church" celebrates a "power that is pure and absolute, which is called the power of right" (5.157). That power, the Confession goes on to say, "the Lord reserves to himself, and does not transfer it to any other" (5.158). This is Christ's power of judgment. No one can claim to usurp this power of separating the sheep from the goats, which belongs to him alone.

There is one power, however, that the Lord does delegate to ministers of the church: the power of the keys (see chapter 12, Ecclesiastical Discipline). Faithfully exercised, this power is "more like a service than a dominion." Indeed, it is akin to the power of a steward of a great household, who holds the keys and decides on behalf of the householder who is admitted and who is excluded (5.159).

Here we have a glimpse into church life of an earlier era, before that rolling snowball of separation between church and state had picked up much

---

Nathaniel Hawthorne's novel *The Scarlet Letter*, set in Puritan New England, exposes the dark side of old-school ecclesiastical power. The tragic image of the adulterous expectant mother, Hester Prynne—forced to stand for hours upon a scaffold in the village square, a scarlet A pinned to her chest—is Hawthorne's protest against the harsh ways the power of the keys was once deployed, dominating New England life. The tremendous popularity of Hawthorne's 1850 novel, reflecting back on the years 1642–1649, indicates the relief with which Americans of his era were casting off what they had come to regard as oppressive ministerial power.

size or speed. In European Reformed communities of the Reformation era, ministers exercised the power of the keys by publicly admonishing church members who, in the minister's opinion, had gone astray in their personal lives of discipleship.

In the Presbyterian Church today, the power of the keys is never exercised by individuals, but only by ordered groups of people, according to the strict guidelines of the Rules of Discipline.

Few powers remain today that are exercised by teaching elders as individuals. When serving as moderators, they are able to call a session meeting or to designate another teaching elder to moderate a session meeting in their absence (G-3.0203, G-3.0201). When serving as pastors, they decide on the Scripture readings, prayers, and musical selections for worship services, as well as the topic of the sermon and any special art forms (such as drama and dance) that may be used in worship to support the proclamation of the Word (W-1.4005). Their personal approval is required when sessions are deciding which hymnal to purchase (W-1.4006). They also decide which couples they will marry, although the scheduling of the church building for wedding ceremonies is a prerogative of the session (W-4.9002b). In certain circumstances, they may exercise powers delegated to them by the session—such as conducting performance evaluations for church staff members—but such powers are only provisional, exercised under the oversight of the session.

General Powers of Councils

By far the greatest portion of the church's ministerial and declarative power is lodged in councils. The section on "Ecclesiastical Jurisdiction," G-3.0102, lists some general responsibilities of councils, making it clear that these are carried out within the limits of "truth and service, order and discipline":

> Councils of this church have only ecclesiastical jurisdiction for the purpose of serving Jesus Christ and declaring and obeying his will in relation to truth and service, order and discipline. They may frame statements of faith, bear testimony against error in doctrine and immorality in life, resolve questions of doctrine and discipline, give counsel in matters of conscience, and decide issues properly brought before them under the provisions of this Book of Order.

Councils have significant freedom to organize themselves to carry out their work, as their particular mission dictates. A barebones organizational structure is specified in the Book of Order, but beyond those mandatory provisions, councils may work out their own pattern of governance. Councils are required to assemble manuals of administrative operations that describe their particular structure and procedures. Such manuals are required to include a sexual misconduct policy and policies on child protection (G-3.0106).

Councils are required to maintain property and liability insurance (G-3.0112). They are also required to prepare and adopt a budget and to keep adequate financial records (G-3.0113). Part of that responsibility is to see that a "full financial review" is conducted each year. This is not necessarily a full-fledged audit conducted by a certified public accountant, although at the very least it must be performed by a committee of people who are independent of the treasurer.

A council is permitted to delegate some of its responsibilities "to such entities as it deems appropriate, provided that those entities remain accountable to the council" (G-3.0106). Generally this is done through committees and commissions, as described in G-3.0109. It is important to understand the difference between the two.

Committees "study and recommend action or carry out decisions already made by a council" (G-3.0109). Committees investigate issues, then return to the council that created them with specific recommendations for the council's action. As part of their report, committees may ask the council to empower them to carry out some of those recommendations.

Commissions have considerable more autonomy. "A commission is empowered to consider and conclude matters referred to it by a council" (G-3.0109). When councils assign tasks to a commission, it is highly important that they "state specifically the scope of the commission's powers and any restrictions on those powers." Within the parameters of those instructions, commissions are empowered to act, and when they do so, they act with the full authority of the council (G-3.0109).

There are two types of commissions, judicial commissions and administrative commissions.

Judicial commissions: Except for sessions (which directly carry out their judicial responsibilities as a committee of the whole) judicial commissions carry out their council's responsibilities under the Rules of Discipline. Their responsibilities are fully described within those Rules (D-5.0000). Unlike other commissions, the decisions of judicial commissions are final (except for appeals that may be filed with the judicial commission of a higher council).

Administrative commissions: Councils may empower administrative commissions to perform a variety of functions. A detailed list of examples is included in G-3.0109b, along with membership and quorum requirements. Chief among these are ordination/installation commissions, examination commissions, commissions to organize new congregations, and commissions to mediate congregational conflicts.

It is important for administrative commissions to keep full records of their proceedings, which will later be incorporated into the council's

It is the practice of some sessions to convert all their committees into commissions, under the mistaken assumption that only commissions can spend money on behalf of the session without having to get specific authorization for each purchase. This is not the case. Committees are permitted to carry out executive functions—to execute instructions given to them by the session—which may include spending funds assigned for their use from a particular line of the church budget. The key distinction between committees and commissions has to do not with performing actions, but rather with making independent decisions. For example, a Christian education committee can be instructed to spend money to purchase supplies for the Sunday school as needed, including purchasing additional copies of the curriculum already approved by the session. Deciding to adopt a new curriculum—a significant policy decision—is probably not something a committee should do. That decision is more appropriately made by either the session as a whole or by a commission appointed for that purpose.

minutes. When commissions report back to the council the actions they have taken, the council may rescind or amend those actions, just as it may do with any action it has itself taken.

Funding the Work of Councils

Funding for the work of councils comes from several sources (G-3.0106). Sessions have access to offerings contributed by members of the congregation. They may also utilize monies obtained from sources such as investment income, rental payments from outside organizations for use of church buildings, and user fees paid by those participating in church programs.

Councils at every other level are likewise dependent on funds from multiple sources. There are few direct contributions by individuals, but there may be income from sales of publications or user fees paid by congregations for consulting services. Endowment income often plays a role as well—particularly at the General Assembly level. By far the most significant source of income for councils, however, comes from two sources: mission and per capita giving.

Mission giving refers to funds contributed by a congregation or council to a higher council. These gifts may be either designated for a certain purpose or undesignated. Presbyteries retain a portion of undesignated mission money for their own programs, forwarding additional portions to the synod and General Assembly, often according to a publicly announced formula.

Per capita giving—which literally means "per head"—is an annual apportionment to cover administrative expenses, paid by presbyteries to the synod and the General Assembly. The amount is based on the number of active church members within the presbytery as of the beginning of the preceding full calendar year. From its beginnings in the earliest days of the church as a common travel-expenses fund for commissioners to the General Assembly, the purpose of per capita funds has grown to cover a variety of administrative needs. At the national level, this includes the expenses of the biennial General Assembly meeting, the Office of the General Assembly and the Office of the Stated Clerk, along with subsidiary offices and agencies.

Unlike mission giving, per capita is not optional—although the council for which it is mandatory is the presbytery, not the congregation. Most presbyteries, in turn, ask the sessions of their congregations to contribute the cost of presbytery, synod, and General Assembly apportionments, based on their active membership totals. In most presbyteries, the amount of per capita funds retained by the presbytery has grown steadily in recent years, to the point that it is several times larger than the amount of the synod and General Assembly apportionments.

While presbyteries may sometimes give the impression that per capita giving is mandatory for congregations, in fact it is voluntary (G-3.0106; G-3.0202f). If sessions fail to remit the full amount of per capita in a given year, the presbytery has no authority to mandate payment. Unless the presbytery reduces its budget, the other churches of the presbytery must make up the difference through increased per capita apportionments in subsequent years. Sessions who withhold all or part of their per capita payments fail to take account of the fact that they continue to receive services from the higher councils for which others are paying.

The stated clerk of the General Assembly, in "Advisory Opinion number 9, Per Capita," has instructed the church that, while the *Book of Order*

One way to look at per capita is that it is the Presbyterian denominational utility. Just as congregations must pay their electric bill, they also need to pay for the administrative services they receive from the denomination. No one disputes that utilities are a good thing, but few members are inspired to heights of generosity by a request to help keep the lights on. Thoughtful sessions will realize that, while it may not always be easy for them to see the many ways per capita helps their congregation, in fact it does—which they will better understand the next time they find themselves in an interim period between pastors or when they must turn to the presbytery for help in conflict resolution.

does not mandate per capita payments by sessions, "it also does not provide the right to sessions and congregations to withhold per capita as a form of protest." That document cites a 2004 General Assembly Permanent Judicial Commission decision in *Minihan v. Presbytery of Scioto Valley* (2004, 350, 2161): "Withholding per capita as a means of protest or dissent evidences a serious breach of the trust and love with which our Lord Jesus intends the covenant community to function together."

Many sessions, following their presbytery's example, ask member households to contribute to an annual per capita offering, in an amount equal to the total per capita apportionment times the number of active members in the household. This has given many church members the unfortunate impression that individual per capita contributions are required by the denomination as a form of membership dues. Whether or not sessions conduct an annual per capita offering appeal or simply budget it as an operating expense is up to them.

Minutes and Records

Councils are also responsible for keeping minutes of their proceedings (G-3.0107). In the case of sessions, this is in addition to the membership rolls and registers previously discussed. Minutes are a record of actions taken by a parliamentary body.

Strictly speaking, minutes consist only of motions that have been passed. While the word "minute" sounds like a unit of time, in fact it reflects an alternate meaning of that word: something very small ("minute" pronounced with long vowels and the accent on the second syllable). A minute is the smallest unit of business a parliamentary body enacts, which is a motion. The minutes are simply a list of these individual actions the council has taken.

Minutes include some other details as well, such as the location of the meeting, the hours when it convened and adjourned, and the fact that it was opened and closed with prayer. They include a record of those in attendance and the signature of the clerk, certifying their accuracy.

Just about everything else that has to go into a set of minutes is associated with properly seconded motions that were passed. It is generally not necessary to record who made or seconded motions, nor is it necessary to summarize comments that were made during debate. Vote counts are necessary only in the case of supermajority motions (those requiring a two-thirds or three-fourths vote). Failed motions are not included; they have no continuing existence, so there is no need to record them. Certain reports received or approved by the council should go into the minutes—especially, in the case of a session, a church register report listing names and dates of births, baptisms, marriages, and deaths since the last meeting, as well as membership additions and removals.

Clerks have broad discretion to include other items as well—both those likely to be useful to the council as it approves the minutes at the next meeting and items that may have some historical interest far into the future. Generally, though, the standard for minutes is "less is more." The best guideline for clerks is the checklist the next-higher council uses in the annual minutes-review process, which can be obtained from the stated clerk of that council.

Minutes belong to the council, although higher councils have the right of review. Current members of the council should be given access to them, upon request, but beyond that, the council will have to make its own decision as to how widely they are publicized. Because minutes sometimes include confidential material, it is unwise to post them publicly or publish them in a newsletter—although it is useful to publish a list of highlights of major decisions the council has made. Another reason not to publish full minutes (as opposed to a list of meeting highlights) is that, in the unlikely event that the church is the subject of a lawsuit, attorneys for the complainant may seek to mine the published minutes for information they can use against the church.

The Presbyterian Historical Society offers to sessions, without charge, the option of archiving hard copies of session minutes and other records in its climate-controlled Philadelphia storage facility. Many Presbyterian theological seminary libraries offer a similar service (G-3.0107). Because of the rapid obsolescence of electronic storage media, the Office of the General Assembly still recommends that at least one copy of official records be maintained in hard-copy form—although this could change in the future as reliable, archival-quality cloud storage becomes more common. Minutes of church councils are retained in perpetuity, so the storage method chosen must reflect this long-term perspective.

Councils higher than the session must have procedures in place to review the minutes of lower councils under their oversight. Most often this is done annually, although the General Assembly and those synods that meet biennially perform this task every other year. Higher councils have the option of calling for special reviews of minutes of lower councils at any time, and ought to do so if they are notified of an alleged irregularity or delinquency, or if they have other reason to suspect there may be problems (G-3.0108).

Should problems be found that require action on the part of the council being reviewed, the higher council can mandate that such an action be taken. If there are judicial proceedings associated with the situation, it may be that the judgment of the permanent judicial commission hearing the case will include some mandated action. A judicial ruling is not required to mandate corrective action. A higher council can do that by simply passing a motion.

The *Book of Order* has little to say about administrative staff who may be hired by councils. It does not require that councils have staff. They need only have officers—moderator, treasurer, and clerk—in order to fulfill their constitutional and corporate responsibilities. Most councils do employ staff, however, and when they do, it is important that they have personnel policies in place, publishing them in their manual of administrative operations. Policies of inclusion and representation, similar to those governing the election of deacons, ruling elders, and teaching elders, must be followed in hiring staff (G-3.0110).

Specific Powers of Congregations

Of all the councils of the church, congregations have the fewest specific powers. In examining the business that may be brought before a congregational meeting, we have seen that these are generally limited to actions concerning electing officers, calling or dismissing pastors, and approving mortgages and real estate transactions (G-2.0404). As it says in G-1.0101, "The congregation is the basic form of the church, but it is not of itself a sufficient form of the church" (see also G-3.0101). Congregations are not fully the church unless they are in partnership with other congregations and councils. This is the chief difference between presbyterian and congregational polities.

Specific Powers of Sessions

The session's powers are briefly comprehended in this statement: "The session shall have responsibility for governing the congregation and guiding its witness to the sovereign activity of God in the world, so that the congregation is and becomes a community of faith, hope, love, and witness" (G-3.0201).

In an extensive list that follows, the session's responsibilities are laid out in three broad categories that correspond to the Reformed notes of the church (F-1.0303). In order to *provide that the Word of God may be truly preached and heard*, the session does the following:

- provides for regular preaching

- provides a place where "worship, education and spiritual nurture" take place,
- takes the good news out into the community
- promotes ministries of social healing and reconciliation, and
- does ecumenical work.

In order to provide that the sacraments may be rightly administered and received, the session "authorizes celebrations of the Lord's supper and baptism" and exercises "pastoral care among the congregation."

In order to nurture the covenant community of disciples of Christ, the session

- receives and dismisses members,
- manages membership rolls,
- provides programs of "nurture, education, and fellowship,"
- examines and ordains ruling elders and deacons,
- encourages stewardship,
- manages church property,
- directs the ministry of all church organizations and of the church staff,
- leads the congregation in mission, and
- performs judicial responsibilities.

In relating to the presbytery, the session

- elects commissioners to presbytery meetings,
- nominates people for election by the presbytery to serve higher councils,
- maintains communications with presbytery,
- proposes measures that may be useful, and
- submits statistics and reports (G-3.0202).

It is through the presbytery that the session relates to higher councils.

Sessions must meet at least quarterly under the leadership of their pastor or other appointed moderator, although most meet monthly. Sessions are not permitted to meet without either a moderator appointed by the presbytery or a substitute moderator designated by their current moderator (G-3.0104). Any items of business may be considered at these stated meetings, although at special meetings, only business specified in the call to the meeting may be considered. Sessions determine their own quorum (G-3.0203).

We have already discussed sessions' responsibility for membership rolls and registers in chapter 6, under the Second Historical Principle. These are detailed in G-3.0204.

Section G-3.0205 fleshes out sessions' financial responsibilities, beyond those already specified in G-3.0113 (a list of general financial responsibilities for all councils). Here are found additional instructions for electing a treasurer and for receiving periodic reports from other entities within the congregation that manage their own funds. The finances of all entities within the congregation are under the session's overall supervision. Several specific requirements for local-church financial management are detailed here:

> a. all offerings shall be counted and recorded by at least two duly appointed persons, or by one fidelity bonded person;
> b. financial books and records adequate to reflect all financial transactions shall be kept and shall be open to inspection by authorized church officers at reasonable times;
> c. periodic, and in no case less than annual, reports of all financial activities shall be made to the session or entity vested with financial oversight.

Congregations are required to be incorporated as nonprofit entities according to the laws of their state, and the session is responsible for seeing that the congregation's corporate status is kept current (G-4.0101). Depending on state law, this may require some kind of annual registration-renewal process, which ought to be carefully monitored. Maintaining active corporate status is important because, under certain circumstances—depending on state law—if the congregation's corporate status is permitted to lapse, session members could be held personally liable in the event that the congregation is sued in the civil courts.

Unless state law dictates otherwise, the corporation is governed by a board of trustees. Ordinarily, members of the session also serve as members of the board of trustees (G-4.0102). This is known as the unicameral (literally, one-room) system. The church treasurer ordinarily serves as the corporate treasurer, and the clerk of session as the corporate secretary. The president and vice president are ordinarily two session members (other than a pastor or associate pastor) elected by the session. Annual and other corporation meetings typically take place in conjunction with congregational meetings—either simultaneously or just after, as state law may dictate. The trustees president, rather than the session moderator, chairs the corporation meeting. In a very small number of congregations—and growing smaller all the time—there is a separate board of trustees, with its members directly elected by the members of the corporation (the congregation), according to a process similar to the way deacons and ruling elders are elected.

Historically, the option to have a separate board of trustees has been the source of endless difficulties—which is why the *Book of Order* considers the unicameral model (merged session and trustees) the default. Even though the *Book of Order* clearly specifies that all entities within the congregation, including the trustees, are accountable to the session, individual trustees have not always found that an easy concept to grasp. Too often a dynamic has arisen in which trustees

Depending on state law, ruling elders under a given age (typically age eighteen) are not permitted to serve as trustees. This does not prevent young people from serving on the session; it simply means that any young people serving on the session are not also trustees.

have come to see themselves as primarily conservators of funds, whose job is to battle the session over any expenditures they consider to be unessential. In the most extreme examples, the board of trustees has accrued such power to itself that the session must come to the trustees each year to request money to fund the church budget: a blatantly unconstitutional practice, since the *Book of Order* gives the session ultimate control over church finances.

The existence of separate boards of trustees is a throwback to an earlier, simpler era in which congregational assets were mostly limited to a sanctuary building and a manse. Building repairs were primarily done by church members themselves, who donated their labor. Frequently, part of the pastor's compensation took the form of in-kind donations such as agricultural produce. Mission funds comprised designated contributions that went directly into a separate benevolence fund. The job of the trustees, in that earlier era, was mostly limited to holding title to the property and overseeing the volunteers who maintained the church buildings. It was not uncommon to see a trustee high up on a ladder, repairing the gutters. Church program expenses were small or nonexistent, with most programming and supplies provided by volunteers. The church budget, therefore, was minimal. Trustees and session members moved in their own separate realms, and rarely was there cause for friction between the two.

By the time church finances entered the twentieth century, they had grown more complex. Over the course of that century, they became vastly more so, with money budgeted for church programming, services provided by contractors and other professionals, multiple salaries and employment benefits, building utilities, insurance policies, office equipment, electronic data services, and a host of other needs. The clear division between session and trustees responsibilities—with the session handling spiritual matters and trustees the temporal—became thoroughly blurred. Conflicts increased. Over the course of that century, increasing numbers of congregations merged their session and their board of trustees, finding it made eminently good sense.

Congregational property is "held in trust . . . for the use and benefit of the Presbyterian Church (U.S.A.)" (G-4.0203).[1] This is true regardless of the language used in the deed of ownership. This situation has been described as analogous to that of a condition or lien placed on a property sale that allows a former owner a "right of first refusal" should the property ever be sold. If the congregation's membership ever dwindles to such an extent that the church must be closed, the property reverts to the presbytery. This also means that any move to sell or encumber (mortgage) any church property requires the explicit prior approval of the presbytery (G-4.0206).

The *Book of Order* places some restrictions on the use of church property. Congregations are not permitted to lease their worship space (sanctuary) to any other group without presbytery approval. They are likewise not allowed to lease any other church property for a term exceeding five years without obtaining presbytery approval (G-4.0206).

Specific Powers of Presbyteries

The most extensive powers in the Presbyterian system are assigned to presbyteries (which is hardly surprising, considering the name "Presbyterian"). Presbyteries are, in fact, the generic council and are stewards of all powers not specifically assigned elsewhere: "The jurisdiction of each council is limited by the express provisions of the Constitution, with the acts of each subject to review by the next higher council. Powers not mentioned in this Constitution are reserved to the presbyteries" (G-3.0101; see also F-3.0209).

This last sentence is of crucial importance as a theoretical construct. It is similar to the Tenth Amendment to the United States Constitution, which states: "The powers not delegated to the United States by the Constitution, nor prohibited by it to the States, are reserved to the States respectively, or to the people." For Presbyterians, congregations may be the primary missional expression of the church, but presbyteries are the primary locus of its governance. Presbyterian governance begins at the presbytery and is delegated to the congregation. That is why, in situations of deep trouble, when presbyteries must move in and replace a session with a presbytery-appointed administrative commission, that action is referred to as "assuming original jurisdiction" (G-3.0306e). As for synods and the General Assembly, those councils do oversee and review the work of presbyteries, but they are delegated bodies with no membership of their own: they are composed entirely of commissioners elected by the primary councils, the presbyteries. Synods and the General Assembly would have

---

1. There are a few congregations from the former Presbyterian Church in the United States that are exempt from this provision. See G-4.0208.

no existence of their own, were it not for the presbyteries who elect their commissioners.

The membership of a presbytery is composed of "all the congregations and teaching elders" within the district it serves (G-3.0301). Looking out over a room where a presbytery is meeting, a newcomer could be forgiven for assuming that the membership of a presbytery is composed of ruling-elder commissioners and teaching elders—but that is incorrect. Ruling-elder commissioners are not members of the presbytery; the *congregations* that elected them are.[2] The only ongoing members of the presbytery are teaching elders and congregations. Ruling-elder commissioners are present to speak for their congregations (although they are still free to vote as guided by their individual conscience).

It is a subtle but highly important distinction. That basic fact of a presbytery's membership shapes nearly everything the presbytery is expected to do. A presbytery's care of its membership has two objects: its teaching elders and its congregations.

Each session elects at least one commissioner to presbytery. Sessions are invited to elect additional commissioners according to a plan the presbytery devises to ensure that meetings demonstrate as even a division (or parity) as possible between ruling and teaching elders (G-3.0301).

After the presbytery has made some change in its minimum terms of call for pastors, some session members have been known to refer derisively to the presbytery as "the ministers' union." That is only half the truth. Presbyteries are concerned with the welfare of their teaching elder members, it is true; but they are equally concerned for the health of the congregations that are also their members.

The presbytery's powers are briefly comprehended in this statement: "The presbytery is responsible for the government of the church throughout its district, and for assisting and supporting the witness of congregations to the sovereign activity of God in the world, so that all congregations become communities of faith, hope, love, and witness" (G-3.0301).

That language is intentionally similar to the general mission statement for sessions (G-3.0201), which likewise have as their goal the creation and maintenance of communities of "faith, hope, love, and witness."

As is also the case with the responsibilities of sessions (G-3.0201), in the

---

2. An exception is ruling elders serving as officers of the presbytery (moderator, vice moderator, stated clerk) who "shall be enrolled as members during the period of their service." A presbytery may, by rule, enroll other ruling elders as members, for the duration of terms pertaining to other elected presbytery service (G-3.0301).

extensive list that follows, the presbytery's responsibilities are laid out in three broad categories that correspond to the Reformed notes of the church (F-1.0303).

In order to provide that the Word of God may be truly preached and heard, the presbytery

- provides for the "organizing, receiving, merging, dismissing, and dissolving" of congregations,
- oversees congregations without pastors,
- establishes and dissolves pastoral relationships,
- oversees the studies and other work of those preparing for ministry,
- maintains ecumenical relationships, and
- encourages congregations in their mission.

In order to provide that the sacraments may be rightly administered and received, the presbytery

- authorizes the celebration of the Lord's Supper at presbytery meetings and for "non-congregational entities meeting within its bounds,"
- authorizes and trains ruling elders commissioned to particular pastoral service to meet the needs of congregations without pastors, and
- exercises "pastoral care for the congregations and members of presbytery."

In order to nurture the covenant community of disciples of Christ, the presbytery

- bears responsibility for "ordaining, receiving, dismissing, installing, removing, and disciplining" teaching elders,
- "commissions ruling elders to limited pastoral service,"
- "[promotes] the peace and harmony of congregations and [inquires] into the sources of congregational discord,"
- assists congregations to develop their financial stewardship,
- develops and promotes mission,
- looks after the members of dissolved congregations and transfers them to existing congregations,
- addresses "error in doctrine and immorality in practice," and
- performs judicial responsibilities.

In relating to higher councils, presbyteries

- elect commissioners to the synod and General Assembly,
- elect readers for standard ordination examinations,
- attend to guidance and communications sent from higher councils and carry out their dictates,
- send overtures recommending action, and
- submit required reports (G-3.0302).

In relating to sessions, presbyteries

- develop regional mission strategy,
- decide on the location of congregations and divide, dismiss, or dissolve them,
- establish minimum compensation standards for pastors and certified Christian educators,
- counsel with them in times of conflict or difficulty,
- recommend appropriate actions,
- mediate disagreements,
- take action to correct problems, as permitted by the Rules of Discipline,
- "assume original jurisdiction in any situation in which it determines that a session cannot exercise its authority," and
- approve leases, mortgages, and sales of congregational real estate (G-3.0303).

More needs to be said about the presbytery's authority to assume original jurisdiction of a congregation, which is one of the most significant and far-reaching powers a presbytery has. The *Book of Order* describes that process in this way:

After a thorough investigation, and after full opportunity to be heard has been accorded to the session, the presbytery may conclude that the session of a congregation is unable or unwilling to manage wisely its affairs, and may appoint an administrative commission with the full power of session. This commission shall assume original jurisdiction of the existing session, if any, which shall cease to act until such time as the presbytery shall otherwise direct. (G-3.0303)

Those in the world of finance are familiar with the phrase "hostile takeover." This action is meant to be benevolent rather than hostile. In fact, it is not a takeover at all, because jurisdiction over a congregation fundamentally belongs to the presbytery and is only delegated to the session. If, after becoming thoroughly familiar with the problems faced by a congregation in crisis, and after conducting one or more hearings at which session members may voice their concerns, the presbytery is convinced no better way forward may be found, it then has the power to relieve the session of its responsibilities, in whole or in part. In that case, the presbytery appoints an administrative commission to carry out the responsibilities of the session. Full assumption of original jurisdiction includes assuming control of church records and financial accounts, managing property, supervising staff, and doing everything else a session would ordinarily do. Sometimes this necessary action takes place over the objections of session members, although there are some cases in which it happens at their own request—if, for example, the session has become so paralyzed by factionalism that decision making has become impossible, or if there have been a great many resignations from the session and the congregation has been unable to elect enough ruling elders to replace them.

Presbyteries must meet at least twice a year, although most meet more frequently. The frequency of presbytery meetings is often a function of geography. Any items of business may be considered at these stated meetings, although at special meetings, only business specified in the call to the meeting may be considered. Presbyteries determine their own quorum (G-3.0304). They keep their own membership rolls and minutes, submitting them periodically to the synod for review (G-3.0305).

Presbyteries exercise pastoral responsibility for their members—teaching elders and congregations—as well as commissioned ruling elders and certified Christian educators serving congregations within their geographic area. They are required to develop procedures to fulfill this pastoral responsibility, as well as to "settle difficulties on behalf of the presbytery where possible and expedient" (G-3.0307).

Behind this flexible, permissive language are hiding two committees that were explicitly required in pre-2011 editions of the *Book of Order* and continue to be used by the vast majority of presbyteries: the committee on preparation for ministry and the committee on ministry.

A *committee on preparation for ministry* traditionally has the responsibility "to guide, nurture and oversee the process of preparing to become a teaching elder," relating to seekers, inquirers, and candidates as they pursue their studies and other preparation (G-3.0307). This committee typically serves as a counselor and advisor on the one hand and as a gatekeeper on the other—two functions that are admittedly in some tension. That tension may be lessened by dividing the work between two subcommittees: a care committee focusing on advice and support and an examinations committee that evaluates candidates and recommends them to the presbytery.

A *committee on ministry* may carry out any or all of these responsibilities, if the presbytery has commissioned the committee to do so:

   –   receive teaching elder members,

- oversee the work of teaching elders,
- approve calls for pastoral service,
- appoint teaching elders or commissioned ruling elders to provide temporary pastoral service,
- oversee congregations without pastors,
- dissolve pastoral relationships,
- dismiss members to other presbyteries,
- annually recommend the validation of the work of teaching elders in nonparish ministries,
- look after the needs of honorably retired teaching elders, and
- maintain relationships with both member congregations and teaching elders (G-3.0307).

As with committees on preparation for ministry, there are different ways the large workload traditionally assigned to committees on ministry may be apportioned among several more specialized committees. Possibilities include a validations committee that determines whether or not teaching elders' work complies with *Book of Order* standards; a vacancies committee that counsels and advises congregations' pastor nominating committees and supports the work of interim pastors; an examinations committee that conducts examinations of teaching elders as they come into the presbytery; a conflict-intervention committee that deploys trained consultants to intervene in congregations in crisis; a small-churches committee that assists and advises smaller congregations served by commissioned ruling elders or various temporary-supply arrangements; a congregational-development committee that coaches teaching elders and sessions on adapting to change; a pastor-to-pastors committee that provides confidential encouragement and support to teaching elders; and an honorably-retired-members committee that focuses on the particular pastoral needs of those faithful servants of the church.

Specific Powers of Synods

It is no secret to anyone familiar with twenty-first-century General Assembly actions that there is a great deal of creative discussion going on concerning the future of synods. A number of factors—declining membership, greater ease of travel, electronic communications, localizing of mission work closer to the grass roots, to name several—have led to a situation in which synods appear to some to have become the proverbial third wheel of Presbyterian governance. Exacerbating that perception is the fact—a feature of Presbyterian polity all along—that synods are out of the loop when it comes to electing commissioners to the General Assembly and ratifying proposed constitutional amendments. Only a few synod functions—notably, permanent judicial commissions that hear appeals of presbytery-level judicial cases and the annual review of presbytery minutes—could not be adequately handled at the national level. In an era of tight denominational budgets, some Presbyterians are concluding that the funds needed to conduct synod assembly meetings could be better used elsewhere.

The *Book of Order* contains a provision for an option known as the "minimal function synod" (G-3.0404). If a majority of presbyteries within the region of the synod so decide, most of the synod's functions may be shut down, with the exception of judicial process and minutes review. The synod assembly could meet as infrequently as every two years, to perform the above-mentioned functions and to oversee whatever minimal budget and staff would be necessary. There is even a provision for sharing judicial function and administrative review across two or more synods.

Powers of the traditional synod are described in G-3.0401–3.0403 and G-3.0405–3.0406. They generally parallel most powers of the presbytery, other than those presbytery powers undergirding relations with congregations and teaching elders.

Specific Powers of the General Assembly

The General Assembly is described as "the council of the whole church." The General Assembly's powers are briefly comprehended in the following statement, whose language echoes the similar statements for each of the councils below it: "The General Assembly constitutes the bond of union, community, and mission among all its congregations and councils, to the end that the whole church becomes a community of faith, hope, love, and witness" (G-3.0501).

The Assembly is composed of an equal number of ruling elders and teaching elders. Presbyteries elect these commissioners according to a formula roughly corresponding to the number of church members in each presbytery (G-3.0502). The precise number of General Assembly commissioners varies from meeting to meeting.

As is also the case with the responsibilities of the councils below it, the General Assembly's responsibilities in the list that follows are laid out in three broad categories that correspond to the Reformed notes of the church (F-1.0303).

In order to provide that *the Word of God may be truly preached and heard*, the General Assembly

- provides for "establishing a comprehensive mission strategy and priorities,"
- maintains ecumenical relationships, and
- conducts the church's global mission work, including sending mission personnel overseas and providing their support.

In order to provide that the sacraments may be rightly administered and received, the General Assembly

- authorizes the celebration of the Lord's Supper at General Assembly meetings and those sponsored by its agencies, as well as at certain ecumenical gatherings, and
- exercises pastoral care throughout the whole church.

In order to nurture the covenant community of disciples, the General Assembly

- provides "those services, resources, and programs performed most effectively at a national level,"
- manages churchwide communications,
- issues study and position papers on a variety of topics,
- addresses "errors in doctrine or immorality in the church and in the world,"
- provides "services of education and nurture as its presbyteries may require"—including curriculum and publishing, among others,
- provides resources to presbyteries in such areas as "mission, prophetic witness, leadership development, worship, evangelism, and responsible administration,"
- discerns "matters of truth and vision that may inspire, challenge, and educate both church and world,"
- performs judicial responsibilities,
- interprets the *Constitution*, and
- maintains the office of the stated clerk—which provides significant services to the church at large that go beyond the work of clerks at every other level (G-3.0501).

The General Assembly's power to interpret the *Constitution* is particularly important. The *Book of Order* describes it as follows:

This responsibility shall include . . . deciding controversies brought before it and advising and instructing in cases submitted to it, in conformity with this *Constitution*; authoritatively interpreting the most recent edition of the *Book of Order* in a manner binding on the whole church, in accordance with the provisions of G-6.02 or through a decision of the General Assembly Permanent Judicial Commission in a remedial or disciplinary case, with the most recent interpretation of the *Book of Order* being binding. (G-3.0501)

This means that, in addition to serving as a legislative body analogous to the Congress of the United States, the General Assembly also performs the judicial functions of the Supreme Court. Sometimes these functions are performed by the Assembly itself as it authoritatively interprets the *Book of Order*, issuing a clarification of what the book means in a particular circumstance, usually in response to a question submitted to it by a presbytery or synod. Authoritative interpretations are subject to review by subsequent General Assemblies, which may amend or rescind them. At other times, it may take the form of judicial process, as questions of interpretation are brought to its Permanent Judicial Commission in the form of remedial cases (D-6.0000).

The General Assembly is required to maintain an Advisory Committee on the *Constitution* to advise it on these matters (G-6.02).

Amending the *Constitution*

There are two different procedures for amending the *Constitution*: one for the *Book of Confessions* and the other for the *Book of Order*.

The procedure for the *Book of Confessions* is the more rigorous of the two,

---

The case law resulting from General Assembly judicial decisions is available to the whole church in the *Annotated Book of Order*, published by the Office of the General Assembly. Rulings of the Permanent Judicial Commission are neither reviewed, amended, nor rescinded by the General Assembly. They are simply received. Because this is a commission of the Assembly, its rulings have the full force of the Assembly itself and are the last word on constitutional interpretation. As with the Supreme Court of the United States, the only way to alter the result of a ruling by the General Assembly Permanent Judicial Commission is to amend the *Constitution*.

---

based on the assumption that confessional documents are not amended frequently, and therefore deserve particular care and scrutiny when they are. The full procedure is outlined in G-6.03, but here is a summary of the main points:

- The General Assembly approves the proposal for church-wide study.
- The General Assembly appoints a "committee of fifteen" to consider the proposal, which reports its findings to the next Assembly.
- The next Assembly considers the report of the committee of fifteen, approves its proposed amendment (perhaps

adding further amendments) and recommends it to the presbyteries.

- Two-thirds of the presbyteries must vote to approve the amendment.
- The next General Assembly approves and enacts the amendment.

While there have been frequent amendments to the *Book of Order* in the past, one purpose behind the most recent revision of the book has been to reduce the need for amendments by moving much of the former detail into locally maintained manuals of administrative operations. Presbyteries and sessions may make their own decisions on such matters, without requiring churchwide debate and vote. Still, there will always be the need for some amendments, and this is how they may be proposed and enacted:

- Proposed amendments, or calls for amendments, must be received by the stated clerk of the General Assembly no later than 120 days prior to the convening of the General Assembly.
- The Advisory Committee on the *Constitution* studies the proposal, reporting its advice to the General Assembly as to its impact on the rest of the *Constitution*, including changes the Assembly may wish to consider.
- The General Assembly approves the amendment and transmits it to the presbyteries for their vote.
- The presbyteries have up to a year after the adjournment of that General Assembly to complete their voting.
- Having received concurring votes from a majority of the presbyteries, the Stated Clerk declares the amendment approved, and it is effective immediately (G-6.03).

Any overture submitted by a presbytery to the General Assembly— whether calling for a constitutional amendment or for any other purpose— requires the concurrence of at least one other presbytery in order to be considered. Synods are under no such restriction.

Chapter 12

ECCLESIASTICAL DISCIPLINE

Lastly, that if the preceding scriptural and rational principles be steadfastly adhered to, the vigor and strictness of its discipline will contribute to the glory and happiness of any church. Since ecclesiastical discipline must be purely moral or spiritual in its object, and not attended with any civil effects, it can derive no force whatever but from its own justice, the approbation of an impartial public, and the countenance and blessing of the great Head of the Church universal. (F-3.0108)

A relatively small number of Presbyterians ever become involved with church discipline, which is as it should be. The intricate legal procedures of the Rules of Discipline are similar to a fire-alarm device whose instructions say: "In case of fire, break glass." As far as most Presbyterians are concerned, that is where these intricate regulations for complaint and grievance are kept: behind glass. Everyone feels relieved to know they are there, but most are thankful if they have never have cause to use them. The Rules of Discipline exist for solving problems that cannot be resolved through ordinary processes of governance—be they procedural complaints or accusations of personal misconduct.

A detailed guide to the Rules of Discipline is found in the *Guide for Judicial Process*, published by the Association of Stated Clerks and available on the General Assembly's Web site. While that document does not have constitutional status, it reflects years of experience implementing the Rules of Discipline, especially at the session and presbytery levels.

An even smaller number of Presbyterians ever experience appeals of decisions rendered under the Rules of Discipline. For that reason, in this book we are focusing primarily on the use of the Rules of Discipline at the session level.

Considering the growing individualism in American society as well as the well-established preference that societal discipline be handled by the secular authorities, the eighth Historic Principle sounds to many like an artifact of an earlier time. It seems almost inconceivable that the somber and even frightening subject of discipline could ever "contribute to the glory and happiness of any church," let alone receive "the approbation of an impartial public." At best, many consider ecclesiastical discipline to be a necessary evil.

That was not how the sixteenth-century Reformers saw it, nor the founders of the Presbyterian Church in the newly minted United States of America. We have already seen how John Knox added ecclesiastical discipline to Calvin's two marks of the church, Word and sacrament. While it may seem incredible that an ex-convict like Knox—survivor of two backbreaking years as a galley slave—would think so highly of discipline, it only goes to show how essential the architects of the Reformation considered church discipline to be.

Once the first-generation Reformers had established their church order, it was not long before they faced threats to their own authority. Luther's suppression of the early Anabaptists and Calvin's refusal to extend mercy to the condemned Unitarian, Michael Servetus, were notable examples. It can be difficult for those who regard centuries-old Protestant denominations as pillars of society to understand that these venerable institutions began their existence in circumstances of societal chaos, in which threats to life itself were daily realities.

Naive observers of post-Colonial American history may likewise assume that, as soon as Lord Cornwallis handed his sword to General Washington at Yorktown, the institutions of an ordered civil society simply continued under the new republic. The years following the Revolution were fraught with chaos and uncertainty. Approximately half a million people (one-sixth of the population of the thirteen colonies) were people of royalist sympathies. As many as 60,000 of them emigrated, mostly to Canada or the British Isles. Numbered among those expatriates were many who had held important positions in government or law enforcement.

Colonial legislatures, who had functioned in a mostly advisory capacity to the royal governors, had to reinvent themselves as agents of governance for the states. By the time the Historic Principles were being written, following the failed experiment of the Articles of Confederation, Knox's concept of discipline had become an even more-sought-after ideal.

The eighth Historic Principle contains echoes of the first ("God alone is Lord of the conscience") in highlighting the separation of church and state. When it declares that ecclesiastical discipline is "purely moral or spiritual in its object, and not attended with any civil effects," it makes it clear that the judgments of church courts are not to be reinforced by civil penalties, nor should church authorities be expected to help carry out sentences issued by secular judges. If a particular offense leads to criminal charges in the civil realm, that proceeding is parallel to ecclesiastical discipline. While ecclesiastical and civil authorities may cooperate with each other in such matters as the sharing of evidence, their respective judicial proceedings are wholly independent of each other. There are many resemblances between church judicial processes and those belonging to civil or criminal law, but there are also some notable differences that may trip up the unwary.

Biblical and Confessional Roots of Church Discipline

In our consideration of the powers of individuals in chapter 6, we mentioned the biblical and confessional concept of the power of the keys. The Heidelberg Catechism grounds ecclesiastical discipline in this concept, which derives from Jesus' naming of Peter in Matthew 16:19 as the rock on which he will build his church.

Although modern biblical scholarship questions the authenticity of this statement as a saying of Jesus—the word *ekklesia*, or church, occurs almost nowhere else in his sayings—there is no question the Reformers considered it to be so (a pair of crossed keys has long been a symbol of Vatican authority as well). In throwing off papal authority, the Reformers felt a burden to articulate clearly who would legitimately hold the keys in their newly created church government.

For a foundational biblical text, they turned to Matthew 18:15–18, which can be regarded as the Rules of Discipline in miniature. As with Matthew 16:19, the occurrence of the word *ekklesia* in this passage—rare in the sayings of Jesus—and the presence of church structures that are evidently more advanced than those of Jesus' informal band of apostles, suggest that this saying reflects the situation of a later generation of the church:

> If another member of the church sins against you, go and point out the fault when the two of you are alone. If the member listens to you, you have regained that one. But if you are not listened to, take one or two others along with you, so that every word may be confirmed by the evidence of two or three witnesses. If the member refuses to listen to them, tell it to the church; and if the offender refuses to listen even to the church, let such a one be to you as a Gentile and a tax collector. Truly I tell you, whatever you bind on earth will be bound in heaven, and whatever you loose on earth will be loosed in heaven.

Binding and loosing, of course, refer to the power of the keys. In response to the question, "What is the power of the keys?" the Heidelberg Catechism supplies this answer: "The preaching of the holy gospel and Christian discipline toward repentance. Both of them open the kingdom of heaven to believers and close it to unbelievers" (4.083).

That Catechism removes the power of the keys from individuals—the pope and those who serve under his authority as priests—and lodges it in the preached Word of God, which has power to convict individuals of their sins. For the recalcitrant who fail to discipline themselves after receiving admonitions from the pulpit, there are formal procedures of ecclesiastical discipline. The Heidelberg Catechism continues:

Q. 84. How does preaching the holy gospel open and close the kingdom of heaven?

A. According to the command of Christ:
The kingdom of heaven is opened
by proclaiming and publicly declaring
to all believers, each and every one, that,
as often as they accept the gospel promise in true faith,
God, because of Christ's merit,
truly forgives all their sins.
The kingdom of heaven is closed, however,
by proclaiming and publicly declaring
to unbelievers and hypocrites that,
as long as they do not repent,
the wrath of God and eternal condemnation
rest on them.
God's judgment, both in this life and in the life to come,
is based on this gospel testimony. (4.084)

This ancient judicial process, set forth in Scripture and confession, is the template for the procedures outlined in the Rules of Discipline. Tenderly and with patient consideration, this biblical teaching encourages those who have been wronged to pursue justice but always to do so with an eye toward reconciliation. At every step in judicial process, opportunities are given for reconciliation. Sometimes these take the form of alternative procedures that—should they prove successful—spare all parties the pain and grief of a formal trial. The goal of the Rules is not punishment but correction, not the destruction of wrongdoers but their rehabilitation. This is clearly seen in the Preamble, the theological foundation statement for all that follows.

Preamble to the Rules of Discipline

The secular courts have their Miranda rights—which, according to a ruling of the United States Supreme Court, must be read to every person who is arrested for a crime. Presbyterian church discipline has its own Miranda rights, of sorts: the Preamble to the Rules of Discipline in D-1.0101, which—according to D-7.0401a—must be read aloud at the start of each ecclesiastical trial.

The power of the keys is implicit from the very first line, which traces the authority for ecclesiastical discipline to Jesus Christ himself. Also present is a description of the restorative purpose of church discipline.

Discipline not only seeks to guide and control but also intends to "nurture" and to provide "constructive criticism."

The Preamble goes on to articulate the separation between civil and ecclesiastical discipline, defining them as unique realms.[3] While the two display similarities to one another, neither secular nor sacred discipline can stand on its own, providing an all-encompassing solution to human sin and error. The two systems are meant to operate with respect for one another's distinctive prerogatives and capabilities.

The remainder of the Preamble's first section contains a long list of specific purposes of the Rules of Discipline:

- *"To honor God by making clear the significance of membership in the body of Christ."* The goal is always to bring people into enhanced relationship with one another in Christ.
- *"To preserve the purity of the church by nourishing the individual within the life of the believing community."* Discipline is meant to meet the needs of the individual while also maintaining the health of the community.
- *"To achieve justice and compassion for all participants involved."* The pairing of these two terms is significant. The hard edge of justice is tempered by compassionate application of disciplinary rulings.
- *"To correct or restrain wrongdoing in order to bring members to repentance and restoration."* The secular judicial system does not always give the highest priority to the rehabilitation of offenders. Although the term "penitentiary" implies a system designed to encourage individuals to come to terms with their guilt and repent, the sad reality is that too often retributive punishment is the only outcome of the court system. The goal of ecclesiastical discipline, by contrast, is not only to call individuals into deeper relationship with their Creator, but also to restore them to the full embrace of the Christian community.
- *"To uphold the dignity of those who have been harmed by disciplinary offenses."* The Rules of Discipline display special concern for those who have been wronged through the sinful acts of others, shielding their anonymity to the greatest extent possible. When they must appear as witnesses, steps are taken to protect them from harassment or retribution.

---

3 See "The Westminster Context: Free Choice within Limits" and "Private vs. Public Judgment," in chapter 5, and "Civil and Ecclesiastical Power," in chapter 11, for more on the separation of church and state.

- *"To restore the unity of the church by removing the causes of discord and division."* Whenever factions develop in the church, the Rules of Discipline are the go-to solution when ordinary means of negotiation and admonition have proven fruitless.
- *"And to secure the just, speedy, and economical determination of proceedings."* Recognizing that time is often the enemy of peace when an alleged offense is publicly known, the Rules are replete with time limits for each stage of the disciplinary process, particularly those related to trials. The fact that most of these time limits are mandatory—and, if violated, can lead to dismissal of the case—ensures that those investigating and prosecuting cases move as quickly as possible through their work.

The Preamble's second section, D-1.0102, goes on to teach that the power of the keys "is one for building up the body of Christ, not for destroying it, for redeeming, not for punishing." Ecclesiastical discipline's ultimate goal is to strengthen the church's life and witness. Always discipline "should be exercised as a dispensation of mercy and not of wrath," so the church can get on with its mission and so all disciples may be led to such repentance that they "may be presented faultless in the day of Christ."

The Rules of Discipline express a healthy sense of their own limitations. The final section of the Preamble, D-1.0103, advises that disciplinary proceedings should not be initiated until all other means have been exhausted. Citing Matthew 5:25—which encourages disciples to reconcile with their accuser on the way to court—the Rules endorse alternative forms of resolution, avoiding trial whenever possible. It is "the duty of every church member" to explore such means before initiating judicial process.

While access to disciplinary process is guaranteed to all Presbyterians as a matter of general principle, the Rules have no patience for the sort of nuisance lawsuits that bedevil the secular court system. Investigating committees may decline to pursue cases if they learn that complainants have rushed to judicial process, skipping over other, more ordinary options that are available to them. Although true nuisance cases are rare in the Presbyterian system, permanent judicial commissions have occasionally refused to hear cases originated by individuals with a track record of habitually using the system to harass others or to advance political goals by judicial means.

Two Principal Types of Cases

The key to understanding the Rules of Discipline is to differentiate between the two principal types of cases and to understand their distinctive terminology. Remedial cases are treated first, followed by disciplinary cases. In between the two is a third type of case: the rarely used request for vindication (D-9.0101), briefly described in half a page.

It can be helpful to envision the structure of the Rules of Discipline as a diptych—the booklike art frame that displays two images side by side, with a hinge connecting the two. On the left is the section dealing with remedial cases, and on the right, the guidelines for disciplinary cases. The hinge is the request for vindication.

Simply put, the difference between remedial and disciplinary cases is that remedial cases address decisions by councils and disciplinary cases address misconduct by individuals. The first question Presbyterians need to ask, when considering initiating a case under the Rules of Discipline, is, "Which type of case is this going to be, remedial or disciplinary?" The answer to that question will dictate where they begin their reading: with chapter 6, which describes how to initiate a remedial case, or chapter 10, which does the same for disciplinary cases.

Both types of cases begin with the filing of a formal statement of the presenting problem. In remedial cases this is called a complaint, and in disciplinary cases, it is a statement of alleged offense—better known as an accusation. Complaints and accusations are filed with the stated clerk of the council that will eventually hear the case.

A quick look at the table of contents reveals that the procedures for trial and appeal in remedial and disciplinary cases are mirror images of one another. The exception is the provision for censure and restoration, which does not apply in remedial cases. In remedial cases, the goal is to determine whether, in fact, a procedural error has been made and then to direct the council that made the error to correct it. The purpose in remedial cases, as

---

Sometimes, in remedial cases, people speak of using the Rules of Discipline to "appeal" an action of a council to the next higher council for review and possible correction. That usage is incorrect. The Rules of Discipline reserve the word "appeal" for the review of judicial decisions alone. The proper term, for this first level of a remedial case, is "complaint."

On the disciplinary side, people sometimes speak of an individual "filing charges" against someone else. That too is a misnomer. A person injured by the actions of another files a "statement of an alleged offense." There are no formal charges until an investigating committee decides to file them, after looking into the situation and deciding if charges are warranted. Only investigating committees have the power to file charges, which lead either to a trial or—with the mutual agreement of all parties—an alternative form of resolution (AFR) proceeding.

the name suggests, is to find a remedy. In filing a complaint, complainants are asked to specify what sort of "relief" they are seeking.

Those initiating a disciplinary case are seeking a guilty verdict on one or more charges. In the event of a guilty verdict, the panel hearing the case—the session (hearing an accusation against a church member) or the presbytery's permanent judicial commission (hearing an accusation against a teaching elder)—must then determine what would, in secular usage, be called a punishment. The word "punishment" is not used in Presbyterian discipline, however, because that word suggests retribution, which is inconsistent with the ideals of rehabilitation and restoration. Neither do the Rules of Discipline speak of "sentencing" offenders. The term of choice is "degree of censure."

Chapter 2, Judicial Process, defines several other general features of remedial and disciplinary cases. First, it reminds all parties that "church discipline is implemented within the context of pastoral care and oversight" (D-2.0101). While this may sound like a surprising way to describe procedures that can result in a painful decision to suspend or remove a person from ordered ministry, it remains consistent with the Preamble's emphasis on "nourishing the individual within the life of the believing community" (D-1.0101). Even censure is seen as beneficial to individuals in the long run, for its goal is to lead them to correct their ways. William Chapman describes discipline as "industrial-strength pastoral care."[4]

Authority of Permanent Judicial Commissions

Ultimately, it is the councils of the church that are responsible for judicial process, although in higher councils, it is not the council itself that conducts the proceeding. Presbyteries, synods, and the General Assembly rely on their permanent judicial commissions to do that work on their behalf (D-2.0102). Only sessions conduct trials themselves, as a committee of the whole. Presbyteries, synods, and the General Assembly perform this function through their permanent judicial commissions. The reason for this is that judicial cases—which permit any member of the trial panel to question witnesses—are best considered by smaller groups. Sessions are themselves a smaller group, but commissioners to presbyteries, synods, and the General Assembly can number in the hundreds.

The decision of a permanent judicial commission carries the full authority of a decision by the entire body. For that reason, appeals are not made to the council that elected them but to the permanent judicial commission of the next-higher council (see D-3.0102). There is no appeal to a decision

4. William Chapman, *History and Theology in the* Book of Order: *Blood on Every Page* (Louisville, KY: Witherspoon Press, 1999), 7.

of the Permanent Judicial Commission of the General Assembly, which is effectively the Supreme Court of the church.

Alternative Forms of Resolution

Chapter 2 also makes a brief reference to alternative forms of resolution (AFR), which are "conducted by professionally trained and certified mediators and arbitrators" (D-2.0103). Note the emphasis here on professional mediators. Neither investigating committees nor sessions nor permanent judicial commissions should ever attempt to conduct AFR proceedings themselves, because this could compromise the objectivity of their judicial roles should the AFR negotiations prove unsuccessful and the case proceed to trial.

Irregularities, Delinquencies, and Allegations

There are two types of remedial cases: those based on allegations of irregularities and those based on allegations of delinquencies. An irregularity is something a council did, but in error. A delinquency is "an omission or failure to act" (D-2.0202). In drawing up a complaint, it is important to use these terms precisely.

Disciplinary cases, by contrast, are based on allegations of an offense. This section defines an offense as "any act or omission by a member or a person in an ordered ministry of the church that is contrary to the Scriptures or the Constitution of the Presbyterian Church (U.S.A.)" (D-2.0303b).

Jurisdiction

Chapters 3 through 5 of the Rules of Discipline cover matters common to both remedial and disciplinary cases. The first of these, covered in chapter 3, is "original jurisdiction," which specifies at which level of governance a case is to be heard.

Sessions have original jurisdiction in disciplinary cases involving members of the church, including deacons and ruling elders (D-3.0101a).

Presbyteries have original jurisdiction in disciplinary cases involving teaching elders who are their members as well as ruling elders they have appointed to serve one of their congregations as ruling elders commissioned to pastoral service (D-3.0101b).

In remedial cases, *the next-higher council* has jurisdiction.

Those who have renounced the jurisdiction of the church, as we have seen (G-2.0407, G-2.0509), cannot be prosecuted under the Rules of Discipline. While a council may decide to make the results of an investigation public in order to provide some sense of comfort and closure to the victims, the statement of renunciation immediately removes a person from both ordered ministry and from membership in the Presbyterian Church (U.S.A.). Consequently, any disciplinary process directed at such a person is immediately halted and cannot proceed any further—although, should the accused ever come under Presbyterian jurisdiction again, the case may be resumed at the point where it was suspended.

Reference

The one-page chapter 4, "Reference," has nothing to do with encyclopedias or dictionaries. It details the ways one council may refer a case not yet heard to the next-higher council (D-4.0101). There are many reasons why a council would want to make such a referral. Disciplinary cases are sufficiently rare at the session level that the ruling elders may conclude that sitting as a court is beyond their expertise. Perhaps, also, the case may engender such strong feelings in the congregation that they fear it could lead to disorder in the church. It may also be that many session members have a conflict of interest. Presbyteries, for their part, may want to refer a case to their synod's permanent judicial commission for similar reasons.

When a permanent judicial commission receives a reference from the lower council, they are under no obligation to accept it. If, after weighing the stated reasons for the reference, they decide it is justified, they will proceed to hear the case. If not, they are required to send it back to the lower council, stating their reasons for doing so and instructing them to hear the case (D-4.0200). There is no appeal to a declined reference such as this.

Permanent Judicial Commissions

Chapter 5 of the Rules of Discipline lays out the guidelines governing permanent judicial commissions. Many of these are of such a detailed nature that they are beyond the scope of this book, but a few highlights are worth noting.

In keeping with the time-honored Presbyterian principle of parity of ministries, presbytery permanent judicial commissions are composed of no fewer than seven members, with equal (or as nearly equal as possible) numbers of ruling elders and teaching elders. Permanent judicial commission members serve the longest term in Presbyterian governance: six years (D-5.0102). Members who have completed a full term of six years may not be reelected to the commission for another four years. Those who have rotated off the commission are still eligible to be called back to sit on judiciary panels should members of the commission have to recuse themselves for that case due to conflict of interest (D-5.0205).

How Remedial Cases Are Filed

Unlike disciplinary cases, which typically involve the testimony of witnesses, evidence in remedial cases is largely composed of documents. Because the complaint is about something a council either did or failed to do, the council's minutes are typically a prime source of evidence. Witnesses may be called, if they can provide useful information beyond that found in the documents.

Remedial cases begin with a written complaint submitted to the council's stated clerk (D-6.0102). The person submitting the complaint is known as the complainant. The council receiving the complaint is known as the respondent.

The complaint may be accompanied by a separate request for a "stay of enforcement," submitted to the clerk of the permanent judicial commission. This procedure requests the commission to prevent the council from carrying out decisions previously agreed upon, pending the outcome of the trial (D-6.0103).

Practically speaking, some decisions can be stayed and some cannot. For example, a decision to terminate a church staff member's employment can often be stayed, allowing the person to keep working while the case is resolved. On the other hand, if the complainant is alleging that the session has published an article in the church newsletter that misrepresents Presbyterian polity, reversing that decision is a matter of trying to get the proverbial toothpaste back into the tube, because the congregation has already read it.

The first thing a permanent judicial commission must do, upon receiving a complaint from its clerk, is to ascertain whether certain preliminary conditions have been met. First, the complainant must have standing to file (D-6.0202). The general rule is that individuals may file a complaint if they are under the oversight of the council; alternatively, other councils may file complaints laterally, against another council on the same level, but individuals belonging to other councils may not.

Pretrial Procedures in a Remedial Case

Next, the permanent judicial commission must ascertain that the complaint contains certain essential elements, including names, the nature of the alleged irregularity or delinquency, the reason for the complaint, and whether there is some relief that can be granted through the judicial process (D-6.0301).

Once these preliminary conditions have been satisfied, the council must elect a committee of counsel of no more than three people to represent it in the judicial proceedings (D-6.0302).

Conditions for Trial in a Remedial Case

If the moderator and clerk of the permanent judicial commission determine that all of the following conditions apply, the case may go forward:

a. the council has jurisdiction;
b. the complainant has standing to file;
c. the complaint was timely filed; and
d. the complaint states a claim upon which relief can be granted (D-6.0305).

If they determine that one or more of these conditions has not been met, the case cannot go forward. If the case does go forward, there are provisions for the council's clerk to copy various parties with documents (D-6.0307) and for the permanent judicial commission to require the parties to file trial briefs summarizing the arguments they intend to make and itemizing the documents they intend to present (D-6.0308).

There is a notable way in which the Rules of Discipline differ from secular law. In the secular realm, there is a process known as "discovery," by which both parties in a case are required to share with each other copies of all the documentary evidence they intend to produce at the trial. There is no such thing as discovery in the Rules of Discipline. Although D-6.0308 requires both parties to itemize their documents by name, there is no requirement that they share copies of the actual documents themselves with the other side prior to trial.

Pretrial Conference in a Remedial Case

Next, the permanent judicial commission schedules a pretrial conference, attended by the complainant and representatives of the respondent's committee of counsel, "to seek agreement on a statement of facts and disputed issues, to exchange documents and other evidence, and to take other action which might reasonably and impartially narrow the dispute and expedite its resolution" (D-6.0310). This is a time at which the possibility of an alternative form of resolution (AFR) may be explored.

Trial in a Remedial Case

Chapter 7 contains detailed instructions for the conduct of the trial before a permanent judicial commission. Most of those details do not concern us here. Anyone retained as legal counsel by either party must be a Presbyterian (D-7.0301). Rules of evidence are detailed in D-14.0000.

During the trial, members of the permanent judicial commission may ask any questions they wish of any participants in the trial. They do not merely sit back and listen while each side presents evidence. This is another example of how trials under the Rules of Discipline differ from trials in the secular courts. The permanent judicial commission is both judge and jury and is empowered to take an active role in determining the truth.

When the testimony is finished, the permanent judicial commission retires to render its decision, which must be recorded in draft written form on the same day the trial is concluded. Copies of the signed decision are distributed to both parties in the case and—in cases beyond the local-church level—to the council to which the permanent judicial commission is related (D-7.0402).

Appeal in a Remedial Case

Chapter 8 describes procedures for appeal in remedial cases. Most of these details do not concern us here, except for the grounds for appeal, which are as follows:

1. irregularity in the proceedings; or,
2. refusing a party reasonable opportunity to be heard or to obtain or present evidence; or,
3. receiving improper, or declining to receive proper, evidence or testimony; or,
4. hastening to a decision before the evidence or testimony is fully received; or,
5. manifestation of prejudice in the conduct of the case; or,
6. injustice in the process or decision; or
7. error in constitutional interpretation. (D-8.0105)

Request for Vindication

With our consideration of remedial cases now concluded, it is time to proceed to chapter 9, the hinge between the two panels of the diptych we have been envisioning as the structure of the Rules of Discipline.

Requests for vindication are neither remedial cases nor disciplinary cases, but something else altogether. This rarely used procedure is a gem embedded in the Rules of Discipline and deserves to be more widely known.

The purpose of a request for vindication is to allow those who believe they have been injured by rumor or gossip to be vindicated by a statement of the truth (D-9.0101). When a request for vindication is filed, the council receiving it proceeds to elect an investigating committee similar to the one they would convene for a disciplinary case (D-10.0201). The difference is that this investigating committee is not asked to consider bringing charges against anyone but rather to listen to all parties concerned and produce a statement of what really happened. This can then be disseminated in such a way as to repair the reputation of the injured party who made the request.

It may be that the investigating committee, after composing its statement of the facts, may become convinced that there ought to be disciplinary charges filed against someone related to the case. In that event, the committee can file charges, initiating a disciplinary case.

Pretrial Procedures in a Disciplinary Case

Because the structure of disciplinary cases closely parallels that of remedial cases, there is no need to repeat those details here. Instead, we will examine how the two types of cases differ from one another.

Generally speaking, disciplinary cases have a much different feel than remedial cases. In cases of misconduct, there are victims who may have been significantly harmed. There are also accused persons who, if in ordered ministry, could potentially lose their ordinations. Sometimes there is an element of scandal of the type of which newspaper headlines are made.

Disciplinary cases begin with a statement of an alleged offense (called, in shorthand, an accusation) rather than a complaint. Three types of individuals have standing to file a statement of an alleged offense:

1. a person under jurisdiction of a council of the Presbyterian Church (U.S.A.) making an accusation against another; or
2. a member of a council receiving information from any source that an offense may have occurred which should be investigated for the purpose of discipline; or
3. a person under jurisdiction of a council of the Presbyterian Church (U.S.A.) coming forward in self-accusation. (D-10.0102)

To some, self-accusation may sound like a strange concept. It certainly is uncommon in the secular justice system. In the church, with its higher moral commitment to the discovery and preservation of the truth, it may sometimes be the case that an individual, through a process of spiritual discernment, has come to feel convicted of his or her own sin and feels compelled to see that justice is done (or, at the very least, to "get it over with," if it seems likely that a statement of alleged offense will be filed).

It should be noted that the restrictions on individuals filing complaints laterally, from a council on the same level, are not present in disciplinary cases. Any member of the Presbyterian Church (U.S.A.), anywhere, may initiate a disciplinary case against any other Presbyterian.

Unlike remedial cases, the investigation phase of disciplinary cases is conducted with a high degree of secrecy. The clerk of a council receiving a statement of alleged offense does notify the session or presbytery that such a statement has been received, without sharing the name of the accused, and asks that an investigating committee be appointed. No further details are provided (D-10.0103). Those being investigated may not transfer membership to another congregation or presbytery until the case has been resolved (D-10.0105).

In situations of alleged sexual misconduct by a teaching elder, the Rules of Discipline require that the clerk communicate to the permanent judicial commission the name of the alleged offender and the nature of the alleged offense. A subgroup of the permanent judicial commission then meets immediately to determine whether or not the teaching elder should be placed on administrative leave, with pay, for the duration of the case (D-10.0106).

Such a decision does make it clear to the congregation or other employing Presbyterian Church (U.S.A.)–related entity that a sexual-misconduct offense has been alleged. No doubt this is an uncomfortable spot for the accused to be in, but the denomination has learned from painful experience that such a move is essential to preserving the peace, unity, and purity of the church.

Presbytery leaders do well to emphasize to congregations that administrative leave is just that, a mandatory procedure in most cases that allows the pastor to concentrate on the details of his or her defense and that presumes neither guilt nor innocence.

Should the investigating committee decide to file charges, it designates one or more of its members to become a prosecuting committee (D-10.0202I). This prosecuting committee assumes a role similar to that of the prosecutor in a secular criminal case, arguing the case before the session or permanent judicial commission. They may be aided by legal counsel.

There is a statute of limitations that prevents charges from being filed based on alleged behaviors that took place more than five years in the past—although there is no time limit in the case of charges of sexual abuse

Typically, both the accuser and the alleged victim are accorded the right "to be accompanied by an advocate at each and every conference . . . with the investigating committee, the prosecuting committee, and the session or permanent judicial commission" (D-10.0203). This advocate is not the same as legal counsel. The advocate's role is to offer personal "support and consultation." This is one way the Rules of Discipline function as a vehicle for pastoral care.

of those under eighteen, those lacking mental capacity, or those who have been the victim of forcible sexual assault (D-10.0401).

The accuser has no official role in a case as it goes to trial, other than responding to questions if called as a witness. "The only parties in a disciplinary case are the prosecuting council and the accused" (D-10.0402b). Having submitted the accusation and supporting evidence to the investigating committee, the accuser has no choice but to trust the prosecuting committee to argue the case.

Trial in a Disciplinary Case

The arrangements for trial are very similar to those for remedial cases. Those accused of offenses are entitled to counsel, which must be provided by a person who is a member of the Presbyterian Church (U.S.A.). The person providing counsel need not be a professional attorney.

As the decision is made, the session or permanent judicial commission is required to determine that the charges on which a guilty verdict is rendered have been proved "beyond a reasonable doubt . . . [which] occurs when the comparison and consideration of all the evidence compels an abiding conviction that the material facts necessary to prove the charge are true" (D-11.0403a). Decisions must be made by two-thirds vote of the session or permanent judicial commission (D-11.0403b).

Censure and Restoration in a Disciplinary Case

If there is a guilty verdict, the session or permanent judicial commission proceeds to hear evidence that may inform its decision as to the degree of censure (D-11.0403e). There are four degrees of censure, ranked from the mildest to the most serious. In the first two, the guilty party retains his or her ordination. In the second two, ordination is removed, either temporarily or permanently:

 - *Rebuke.* This is a stern statement of the offense, with the encouragement not to persist in similar behavior in the future (D-12.0102).

- *Rebuke with Supervised Rehabilitation.* This is similar to a simple rebuke but is accompanied by a program, mandated and monitored by the session or permanent judicial commission, that will encourage the guilty party to avoid similar behavior in the future (D-12.0103). Often, supervised rehabilitation is a program of counseling therapy, but it may also include making restitution or performing work akin to community service in the secular legal system.
- *Temporary Exclusion from the Exercise of Ordered Ministry or Membership.* In this option, the person's ordination or church membership is removed for a period of time, with the end of that period often defined by the successful completion of a program of supervised rehabilitation similar to that described in the preceding option (D-12.0104).
- *Removal from Ordered Ministry or Membership.* This is the most severe degree of censure. Deacons or ruling elders are stripped of their ordination. Church members may be removed from all membership rolls and ordered ministries. Teaching elders have their ordination removed and their pastoral relationship dissolved and are removed from the roll of the presbytery (D-12.0105). There is no rehabilitation. No pathway to reinstatement is outlined, other than the process of restoration.

Restoration, which requires public repentance, may be granted only by the council responsible for imposing the censure (D-12.0201). Even if those seeking restoration have moved to another part of the country, they are required to return to the council of their former membership to apply for restoration—an important protection for the larger church.

Appeal in a Disciplinary Case

Chapter 13 describes how appeals of disciplinary decisions by sessions or permanent judicial commissions may be made to the next-higher council. These appeal procedures closely parallel those in remedial cases, so there is no need to repeat those details here.

Should it happen that all counts on which the accused has been found guilty are reversed on appeal, "it is in effect an acquittal, and the person is automatically restored to ordered ministry or membership in the church" (D-13.0405). The permanent judicial commission sustaining the appeal acts, in such circumstances, as an agent of God's grace and justice.

Evidence in Remedial or Disciplinary Cases

We have already observed how, during the stages after the investigation is completed but preceding the trial, there is no such thing as discovery in the Rules of Discipline. There are, however, rules of evidence, which are enumerated in chapter 14.

Chapter 13

PRINCIPLES OF PRESBYTERIAN GOVERNMENT

Having completed our study of the Historic Principles of Church Order, it remains to briefly examine the list that follows it, the Principles of Presbyterian Government (F-3.02).

Adopted by the General Assembly in 1797, nine years after the Historic Principles of Church Order, the Principles of Presbyterian Government originally took the form of a dense, single-sentence paragraph called the "Radical Principles of Presbyterian Government and Discipline." Today's *Book of Order* breaks that long sentence up into its constituent clauses, assigning to each one a different reference number and providing further detail. The original text may be found in a footnote to F-3.02.

As we have seen, this list differs from the Historic Principles of Church Order in that it deals not with theological concepts of order but with practical procedures of government.

The list begins, appropriately enough, with the church's unity.

F-3.0201—One Church

The particular congregations of the Presbyterian Church (U.S.A.), wherever they are, taken collectively constitute one church, called the church.

What may seem at first to be a rather obvious statement, built on the first classical mark of the church, in fact has far-reaching consequences for the ways in which church councils interact with one another. When members move from one community to another, they join another congregation by means of transfer rather than having to join anew (G-1.0303b). Inquirers or candidates may be transferred from one presbytery to another (G-2.0608). When a person is ordained to an ordered ministry, that ordination is "an act of the whole church, carried out by the presbytery" and is therefore automatically recognized by all other councils (G-2.0701). Under the Rules of Discipline, those with standing to file a complaint or accusation include members of other councils or other councils themselves (D-6.0202; D-10.0102).

F-3.0202—Governed by Presbyters

This church shall be governed by presbyters, that is, ruling elders and teaching elders. Ruling elders are so named not because they "lord it over" the congregation (Matt. 20:25), but because they are chosen by the congregation to discern and measure its fidelity to the Word of God, and to strengthen and nurture its faith and life. Teaching elders shall be committed in all their work to equipping the people of God for their ministry and witness.

The two types of presbyter—ruling elders and teaching elders—when participating in councils higher than the session, always govern together in a relationship of numerical parity (G-3.0301; G-3.0401; G-3.0501). Ruling elders' responsibility to "discern and measure [the congregation's] fidelity to the Word of God" is demonstrated in their responsibility for "warning and bearing witness against error in doctrine and immorality in practice within the congregation and community" (G-3.0201c). Teaching elders' responsibility for "equipping the people of God for ministry and witness" is apparent in the way the Directory for Worship assigns pastors sole responsibility for key elements in the worship service that are related to the proclamation of the Word (W-1.4005).

F-3.0203—Gathered in Councils

These presbyters shall come together in councils in regular gradation. These councils are sessions, presbyteries, synods, and the General Assembly. All councils of the church are united by the nature of the church and share with one another responsibilities, rights, and powers as provided in this Constitution. The councils are distinct, but have such mutual relations that the act of one of them is the act of the whole church performed by it through the appropriate council. The larger part of the church, or a representation thereof, shall govern the smaller.

Here the word "council" is introduced, defined so as to comprise "sessions, presbyteries, synods, and the General Assembly" (G-3.01). It is worth noting that congregations are not councils: a council, by definition, is composed exclusively of presbyters. This means presbyteries do not have direct oversight of congregations, but rather of the sessions that govern them.

The statement about the act of one council being "the act of the whole church performed by it through the appropriate council" provides the basis for the next line that follows, about the larger part of the church governing the smaller. A higher council's oversight of a lower one is focused on witness: councils "nurture, guide and govern those who witness as part of the Presbyterian Church (U.S.A.), to the end that such witness strengthens the whole church and gives glory to God" (G-3.0101). If the product of the church is faithful witness, then councils may be seen as the church's quality-control department.

F-3.0204—Seek and Represent the Will of Christ

Presbyters are not simply to reflect the will of the people, but rather to seek together to find and represent the will of Christ.

This time-honored principle was not part of the 1797 Principles of Presbyterian Government but was imported here, at the time of the 2011 Form of Government revision, from elsewhere in the book. Where this lofty statement of purpose finds practical application is in the methods councils use to elect commissioners to higher councils.

In secular government, it is common for the electorate to expect their representatives to support their majority interests. If a majority of the electorate is calling for a particular legislative measure, then the representative is expected to work energetically to achieve it. In the Presbyterian Church, by contrast, councils are forbidden from instructing those they elect on how to vote on measures coming before the higher council. The reason for this is that each council seeks the guidance of the Holy Spirit through the process of parliamentary debate. If commissioners arrive at the meeting having already determined how they are going to vote, they are not opening themselves up to the Spirit's further guidance.

Presbyterians do not use the word "representatives" to describe those they elect to serve in this fashion. Rather, we call them "commissioners"—indicating that those elected to the higher council are given full authority to speak and vote on the lower council's behalf, under the guidance of the Spirit.

F-3.0205—Decision by Majority Vote

Decisions shall be reached in councils by vote, following opportunity for discussion and discernment, and a majority shall govern.

It may seem surprising, to some, to learn that the Presbyterian Church was not governed by *Robert's Rules of Order* at the time of its founding. The first edition of that book was not published until 1876, when US Army Colonel Henry Martyn Robert, after a bad experience presiding over a chaotic church meeting, published his book of suggested parliamentary rules for voluntary organizations. Robert adapted his rules from those then in use in the US House of Representatives.

Those rules, in turn, had deep roots in British parliamentary law. So, although *Robert's Rules* was still nearly a century away at the time of the denomination's founding, majority rule was certainly well known to its founders. There is nothing magical about the "50 percent plus one" that constitutes a majority. It is by allowing space for the Holy Spirit to act, through faithful discussion and prayerful discernment, that a council may be so bold as to claim it is expressing the will of God for that place and time.

F-3.0206—Review and Control

A higher council shall have the right of review and control over a lower one and shall have power to determine matters of contro-versy upon reference, complaint, or appeal.

The relationship between a higher council and a lower one moves in two directions. The relationship flows from higher to lower thorough certain regular opportunities the higher council has to conduct reviews—most notably, the annual or biennial review of minutes (G-3.0108a) and such decisions a council may make to send representatives to visit the lower council. In the event that a higher council becomes aware of a particu-lar problem, it can initiate a special administrative review, sending an administrative commission to review records, speak with individuals, and report back with action recommendations (G-3.0108b). A higher council can direct a lower council to correct practices deemed to be improper, either by order or through judicial process (G-3.0108c). Approaching from the opposite direction, a lower council may submit a remedial case to the next-higher council, asking for a formal ruling on a particular point of controversy (D-6.0202).

F-3.0207—Ordination by Council

Presbyters (ruling elders and teaching elders) and deacons are ordained only by the authority of a council.

In contrast to churches with an episcopal polity—in which ordination authority is vested personally in a bishop—Presbyterians who are called to ordered ministry are ordained only by the authority of a council. In the case of deacons or ruling elders, this is a session (G-2.0403; W-4.4000). In the case of teaching elders, it is a presbytery (G-2.07; W-4.4000). Presbyter-ies performing ordinations are functioning as a corporate bishop. In either case, it is important to view the laying on of hands not as the passing-on of a personal ordination charism from one or more already ordained persons to another but rather as an act of corporate worship, with the personal involvement of session or presbytery members being necessary for the sake of good order.

This is why deacons do not ordinarily take part in the laying-on of hands at the ordination of fellow deacons: it is something ruling and teaching elders do as part of their governance responsibilities. Some sessions may ask deacons to participate in the laying-on of hands, but they should make it clear that this practice is, for the deacons, an act of prayer, not an act of governance.

F-3.0208—Shared Power, Exercised Jointly

Ecclesiastical jurisdiction is a shared power, to be exercised jointly by presbyters gathered in councils.

Ecclesiastical power in general is primarily exercised by councils rather than individuals. For obvious historical reasons, Presbyterians have a native distrust of ecclesiastical power exercised by individuals. This is why Presbyterian polity primarily limits the individual decision-making power of teaching elders to a few matters related to the planning and oversight of worship (W-1.4005). Virtually every other decision in a local congregation is made by the session.

Similarly, the moderator's tenure in presbyteries, synods, and the General Assembly is traditionally of short duration, typically one to two years—although the exact length of the moderator's term is left to the council to decide (G-3.0104). In the event that councils hire administrative or executive staff, their role is to carry out the council's mandates rather than to act individually in an episcopal fashion (G-3.0110).

When a council needs to visit a lower council or congregation under its oversight, this is done by means of an administrative commission (G-3.0109b). In the case of formal judicial action, the permanent judicial commission steps in (G-3.0109a; D-5.0000). In both cases, it is the action of a group rather than an individual.

F-3.0209—General Authority of Councils

Councils possess whatever administrative authority is necessary to give effect to duties and powers assigned by the Constitution of the church. The jurisdiction of each council is limited by the express provisions of the Constitution, with powers not mentioned being reserved to the presbyteries.

This final Principle of Presbyterian Government is of far-reaching importance. With the exception of presbyteries, any administrative authority exercised by councils is limited to that specifically assigned to them by the *Book of Order*. Presbyteries, however, exercise not only the powers assigned to them, but also any other power not specifically allocated to another council.

An ancient Latin proverb attributed to Augustine, *Ubi Christi, ibi ecclesia*, is translated as "Where Christ is, there is the church." While no Presbyterian would quibble with that statement, when it comes to specifically Presbyterian church governance, the proverb could be alternatively stated: "Where the presbytery is, there is the Presbyterian Church."

This is a clear expression of the concept of "connectional church." For Presbyterians, ecclesiastical power neither rises up from below (congregational polity) nor trickles down from above (episcopal polity). It originates in this essential midcouncil of the church: a place where, by the inspiration of the Holy Spirit, individual leadership talents may shine and decision making may be tempered by the wisdom of the community.

AFTERWORD

In this book we have pursued an inductive approach to studying the *Book of Order*, emphasizing "first things first," the foundational principles on which all else is based. We have seen how the eighteenth-century principles of polity that led to the creation of the first book are still highly relevant today, once allowances are made for the ways the English language has changed over the centuries.

Perhaps it is best to conclude by recalling the final lines from the eighth Historic Principle, "The Value of Ecclesiastical Discipline." This closing observation about discipline is just as true of church order in general. At the end of the day, church order "can derive no force whatever but from its own justice, the approbation of an impartial public, and the countenance and blessing of the great Head of the Church universal" (F-3.0108). As long as we keep those limitations in mind, remembering that order is God's gift for the upbuilding of the church, we Presbyterians will continue to value the *Book of Order* as an essential tool for mission and ministry.

INDEX OF *BOOK OF ORDER* REFERENCES

CPSIA information can be obtained at www.ICGtesting.com
Printed in the USA
LVOW11s0328030316

477527LV00001B/24/P